The Adve

John Patterson

With Notices Of The Officers, &C. Of The 50Th, Or Queen's Own Regiment, From 1807 To 1821

John Patterson

Alpha Editions

This Edition Published in 2021

ISBN: 9789354508189

Design and Setting By
Alpha Editions
www.alphaedis.com
Email – info@alphaedis.com

THE ADVENTURES OF CAPTAIN JOHN PATTERSON,

WITH NOTICES OF

THE OFFICERS, &c.

OF THE 50th,

OR

QUEEN'S OWN REGIMENT,

FROM

1807 TO 1821.

LONDON:
T. & W. BOONE, 29, NEW BOND STREET.

1837.

TO

THE QUEEN'S

MOST EXCELLENT MAJESTY.

MADAM,

Encouraged by the very flattering manner in which your Majesty condescended to present the 50th with the Colours which they now carry, as well as by a high sense of the honour conferred upon the Regiment when they were styled the "Queen's Own," I have presumed to dedicate to your Majesty this feeble record of their services during the late War.

I am fully assured that in whatever quarter of the globe their colours may be displayed, it will be to gain new honours in the field, and that, therefore, the Regiment will ever maintain that place in your Majesty's favour, which they have had the singular good fortune to acquire.

I have the honour to be, Madam,

Your Majesty's most obedient,

and very faithful Subject,

JOHN PATTERSON,

CAPTAIN,

Late of the 50th, or Queen's Own Regiment.

Liverpool,
25th October, 1836.

TABLE OF CONTENTS.

CHAPTER VI.

CHAPTER VII.

CHAPTER VIII.

CHAPTER IX.

CHAPTER X.

CHAPTER XI.

CHAPTER XII.

CHAPTER XIII.

CHAPTER XIV.

CHAPTER XV.

CHAPTER XVI.

CHAPTER XVII.

CHAPTER XVIII.

CHAPTER XIX.

CHAPTER XX.

CHAPTER XXI.

ERRATA.

Page 6, 8 lines from bottom, for "queses," read "cues."
12, 5 for "groops," read "groupes."
40, 2 for "60th," read "50th."
46, 12 lines from bottom, for "among wood," read "among the wood."
48, In the list of killed, &c. at Vimerio, instead of the passage printed, read "Capt. A. G. Coote, killed; Major Charles Hill, and Lieutenant J. N. Wilson, wounded."
60, 4 lines from bottom, for "blackening," read "blanching."
135, 9 lines from bottom, for "throgout," read "throughout."
149, 4 for "Cajo," read "Caio."
192, 5 lines from top, for "wood," read "mood."
199, 6 for "Chandler," read "Candler."
203, 4 for "Thril," read "Thiele."
221, 6 lines from bottom, for "mach," read "march."
265, 2 lines from top, for "firm," read "fine."
314, 2 lines from bottom, for "70th," read "71st."
344, 11 for "settimo," read "septimo."
352, 5 lines from top, for "Lieutenant General Bentley, Lieutenant General Power," read "Lieutenant George Bartley, Lieutenant Power."
352, at the top, for "Lieutenant and Adjutant D. Mc Donald," read "Lieutenant Duncan Mc Donald."
390, 2 lines from bottom, for "Wailey," read "Warley."
389, 3 lines from top, instead of "to behold with what vanity as well as delight not a few," should read, "to behold with what delight as well as vanity not a few."

ADVENTURES.

CHAPTER I.

It seems to be a general custom for the retired soldier, after he has sheathed his now harmless blade, to wield the pen, and, looking back upon his past campaigns, deliver "a round unvarnished tale." I have no wish to be singular, by making myself an exception to the rule; on the contrary, I am rather desirous of appearing on the list of those who fight their battles o'er again. I shall, therefore, as a young recruit, take part among the troop of scribblers; and, without any unnecessary preamble, assign one reason for my embarking in the cause.

Among the various military narratives, written to edify the world, nothing has yet transpired regarding the old Fiftieth; not a single champion has been bold enough to step forward, and say a word or two in favour of that corps. Now, as the battalion, whenever the pebbles were flying about, was never in the back ground, there can be no excuse for silence upon the subject. Moreover, the high esteem in which I hold the companions of many a hard fought day prompts me to offer this feeble record of their services, so far as I have witnessed them; and, at the same time, to endeavour to rescue from oblivion, the memory of those brave men, who fell for their country. It perhaps may be asserted, that the interest in all such matters is now gone by, and that it is a hackneyed, dry, and threadbare theme; but I must beg leave to differ from those sapient persons, who perchance may entertain this notion.

The scenes in this eventful war were ever changing; each performer ran a career as varied as the clime or country through which he travelled; in fact, so diversified were the circumstances, that if every individual from the drum-boy upwards, were to write his own adventures, I am well convinced, the story would not be wholly devoid of interest, because it would at least have novelty to recommend it.

As for the movements and operations of the army, in the Spanish peninsula, they have been already well described by Colonel Napier; and therefore I consider that any account, even from the most talented pen, would be superfluous, after the details which have been so clearly given by that able historian.

The hurried nature of our service rendered it impossible for us to see beyond the surface. We were scarcely ever allowed to remain more than a day or two, in any town worthy particular notice. The woods and wilds were generally the places of our habitation. From this cause, description will necessarily be meagre, and little more than an unfinished sketch, or outline, can be looked for. I shall confine myself to things that fell within the range of personal observation, many of which were noted down in a journal at the time; and in doing so I may hope to introduce some gleanings, not wholly worthless, that may have escaped the cognizance of others more experienced, and who even were long before me in the field. If the general reader should deem my preliminary matter to be of minor importance, I must beg to remind him, that there are many veterans to whom it will appear in a different light; and I must solicit his patience till I can lead him into more stirring scenes.

Having, in August 1807, received a commission in his Majesty's 50th, or West Kent regiment, I joined the 2nd battalion of that corps, commanded by Lieutenant-Colonel Charles Stewart, at Deal barracks, on the 17th of the following month. It was composed chiefly of young recruits and of volunteers from the English Militia, and was undergoing a strict course of drill; the whole of the officers and men being diligently employed in practising the manual and platoon exercise, marching, countermarching, and the balance step.

Lieutenant-Colonel Stewart, who had lately

been promoted from the 53rd, in which he had served for some years, was an old and very distinguished officer, having encountered the vicissitudes of war, in almost every quarter into which the British arms were carried. In the East Indies, while present at the siege of Seringapatam, as Captain of the 71st Highlanders, he bore a conspicuous part, when leading his company to the assault of that fortress, in which he was severely wounded. He was a hardy Northern, skilled in martial science, and was as eminent in those qualities which are required for training up the young battalion as for those which are displayed in manœuvring the more experienced in the field. His hoary locks, well blanched by many a hard campaign, indicated the length of service to which his best days had been devoted, while his penetrating expression of countenance indicated the active mind, and the abilities, by which he was so highly distinguished.

In the adjoining barrack lay the 29th or Worcestershire regiment, commanded by Lieutenant-Colonel Daniel White. It had lately returned from Halifax, where it had been stationed for many years.—Being in preparation for active employment, it was now passing through the usual ordeal of drill and ball practise; and consequently the interminable sounds of drums, and bugles, the monotonous dïn of the drill serjeants' "as you were," accompained by the clamour from the Adjutants' stentorian lungs, were continually wringing in our ears.

The 29th was a fine regiment, although it had been trained up after the manner of the old school. Their Lieutenant-Colonel, a gallant veteran,* shewing the example, made his officers dress with cocked hat square to the front, long queses, and wide skirted coats, fastened or looped back with hook and eye—They had rather too much of the antique about them, and were considerably improved by getting into a more modern style of costume.

We were enlivened by their excellent band;

---

* This fine old officer was killed at the battle of Talavera, while nobly leading his regiment to the charge.

and their corps of black drummers cut a fierce and remarkable appearance, while hammering away on their brass drums. This regiment, when complete, was sent to Portugal, where by its good conduct it acquired as large a share of laurels as any other in the Peninsular army.

The 2nd battalion of the 50th marched, on the 8th of October, 1807, to the town of Ashford in Kent, at which place we had excellent accommodation and good barracks.

An order soon after arrived for a draught, consisting of one Captain, two Subalterns, and 150 men, to proceed forthwith to join the 1st battalion, then on its route to Portsmouth. The detachment left Ashford on the 16th of November, under the command of Captain H. I. Phelps.*

The 1st battalion of the 50th, or West Kent regiment, commanded by Lieutenant-Colonel George Townsend Walker, was, at that time,

* Captain Phelps, was shortly after exchanged into the 80th and consequently was not among the number who embarked with the 1st battalion.

above a thousand strong, having been completed by men from the second battalion, on its return from the expedition to Copenhagen. In addition to the old hands, they obtained a full supply of young active fellows, who had volunteered from the English Militia,—the whole, officers as well as privates, were in good health and spirits, elated with the prospect of active service, and looking forward to new adventures as well as to encountering the enemy in the field. But it was not alone by numerical strength or physical power that the 50th was likely to be formidable. There was likewise an "esprit de corps," a high tone of feeling among them, producing a moral force not easily to be overcome.

When, after a long and harassing route, on a dismal wintry day in October, the men marched up the main street in Hythe covered with mud, drenched with rain, their clothing and accoutrements tarnished, their black facings in good keeping with their dingy costume, they certainly looked more like a band of demons than human beings, and realized, on this occasion at least, their ancient pet appelation of the 'dirty half hundred.'

The 50th has undergone several changes of name, both serious and ludicrous. At the period of which we are writing, it was the West Kent regiment. When, after its return from the West Indies, in 1827, it received a new set of colours, at Portsmouth, from the hands of Queen Adelaide, (then Duchess of Clarence) it became the 'Duke of Clarence's.' On our present gracious sovereign's accession to the throne it was made a royal regiment, and obtained the honor of being styled the 'Queen's Own,' which is its present name. Among military men, it has been known by various jocose titles; at one time it was called the 'Mediterranean Greys,' from its having been so long on that station that the locks of men and officers had assumed a grisly hue. It was, at another period, named the 'Blind Half Hundred,' from being so much afflicted with the ophthalmia in Egypt. The 'Old Black Cuffs,' and the 'Dirty Half Hundred,' from the dingy colour of the facings, are still favourite appellations.—But let us resume our march.

We arrived at Portsmouth on the 26th of November, 1807, having had a toilsome march of ten days; the roads were bad, and the weather was unusually cold and wet; so that we did not make a very respectable or beautiful figure, upon our entrance into that garrison, any more than we did at our exhibition in Hythe. The object of our coming to Portsmouth, was to form a portion of an expedition which was to assemble at this place of rendezvous, preparatory to its embarkation for a destined quarter, to what part of the world it was to direct its course was, however, as yet unknown to the troops who were to be engaged in it.

The force to be employed on this secret enterprize consisted of the following regiments, viz.:—

The 29th regiment, Lieut.-Col. White.

The 32nd regiment, Lieut.-Col. S. V. Hinde.

The 50th regiment, Lieut.-Col. G. T. Walker.

The 82nd regiment, Lieut.-Col. Sir G. Smith.

The Armament was to be under the orders of Major General Sir Brent Spencer, an officer of well-tried experience, and merit, who had signalized himself on many occasions, and particularly when leading forward the old 40th on the sands of Egypt. With such a gallant chief at our head, followed by such troops, we could not fail to be inspired with confidence, that to whatever quarter the expedition might be bound, success would inevitably attend upon our arms.

Previous to our going on board, a limited number of women were allowed to accompany the regiment, and lots were cast in order to decide this very delicate affair.—It was most affecting to witness the distress of those whose fate it was to remain behind, and the despair that was pictured on the countenances of the unhappy creatures was truly pitiable.—Many of them young, helpless, and unprotected, were forced to wander back to their own country, pennyless, and broken-hearted, and to all intents and purposes left in a widowed state, for few of them were fated ever to behold their husbands again.

The moment of separation was a painful one, and was calculated not only to touch the hearts of the most indifferent observer, but to affect most deeply those who, while they felt for the mourners, had no power to mitigate their sorrows.

The embarkation took place on the 17th of December. The troops were assembled on that spot, well known by the name of Portsmouth point, a place which, albeit it possesses but a scanty portion of the picturesque, even now furnished with a goodly display of animated nature, and covered with groups of motley garb and colour, consisting of all the rank, beauty and fashion of that very polite and elegant quarter of the town, drawn hither from their saloons, to witness the departure of the soldiers.

CHAPTER. II.

The whole of the troops being on board, the fleet got under way, from Spithead, with a fine breeze from the E. N. E. and stood down channel for the westward.

The transports fitted up for our reception, were small vessels of such old and crazy materials, that in this wintry season, we did not expect they would long remain sea-worthy. However as we were now commencing the uphill work of a soldier's life, our minds were fully made up to rough it in every sense of the word; and, although appearances were not flattering, our feelings were in unison with the motto on our breast-plate, (quo fata vócant) and we were buoyed up with the hopes of a prosperous issue to our undertaking.

Captain Bentley's company, (to which I belonged) was stowed in the brig Alexander; she was an old tub, battered and knocked about by many a gale, and in her look and trim was by no means inviting.

The skipper, Captain Young, a tall, hard-featured seaman, with a countenance well bronzed by exposure to the N. W. wind, was positive and irritable to an extreme degree, and if a landsman presumed to offer any remark, as to the affairs of his beautiful ship, Old *Young*, was quite indignant.

We were fortunate in getting Bentley for a shipmate, as he was a kind good tempered man, and a lively companion.

The pay-master, John Montgomery, with his wife and family, were also of our party ; so that on the whole, we in the Alexander were as well off with respect to society, as any of our neighbours. Montgomery was a plain, good-natured Irishman, fond of social life, and being a man of experience, having spent most of his days in the regiment, he was an acquisition, which ultimately proved valuable to us. His eldest daughter, an animated sensible girl, contributed with two younger sisters to our happiness ; and, making due allowance for the state of things around, we had as large a share of enjoyment, (if such a word can be used with reference to being in a ship), as under the circumstances could reasonably be expected.

The fleet was soon clear of the channel, bearing on a S. W. course, under a heavy press of canvass, before a fair wind.—The appearance of the clouds and atmosphere was unfavourable, and the huge unwieldy porpoises, rolling about their shapeless forms, together with the screaming of mother Cary's chickens, were to the experienced mariners certain indications of a coming storm. Their evil prognostics were soon realized; for, on approaching the Bay of Biscay, we were driven and tossed about, by one of the most violent tempests that had occurred for many years.—It began on Christmas day. Resolving to enjoy, though in a humble way, the good cheer of the festive season, we had previously provided for the occasion a fat goose, and other savoury things; but, alas, our promised joys proved deceptive; they all vanished, and were replaced by sorrow and disappointment, for the relentless gale denied all possibility of comfort! Poor blackey, in his caboose, was rendered inconsolable, he being unable to dress the aforesaid goose, as the spray, beating in, had quenched the last spark of his culinary fire. The ship reeled and pitched with such tremendous force, that it was not without some trouble we could discuss the merits of a cold bone of junk with hard biscuit, while we lay sprawling and floundering on the wretched cabin floor. The dead-lights having been previously fixed to the stern windows, there remained but the flickering and moody glare of a yellow dirty looking luminary, y'clept a lamp, which, as it swung from the sky-light grating, afforded a glimmering just sufficient to make darkness visible, and disclose to our visual organs a scene emphatically dismal.

Such was the commencement of our calamitous voyage, and in this way did we get on, from bad to worse, each day more woeful than the preceding; until at length, after beating about this Bay of Misery, against a strong head sea, and with a hurricane in our teeth, it was thought advisable to fight no longer with the elements; the signal was therefore made from the Commodore, to tack about, and make sail for England.—Obeying this welcome signal with alacrity, we found ourselves going homewards before the wind, at the rate of from ten to twelve knots an hour, after having been exposed to its dreadful violence for the space of ten days, in the most terrific sea that any unfortunate bark had ever ploughed.

At this time, as we looked across the foaming waste, the view was wild and dreary; amidst the atmosphere of darkness, clouds and mist, the scattered vessels might be occasionally discerned, as the fog dispersed, tossed about at the merciless fury of the waves; some dismantled, others on their beam ends. The wrecks of those that unhappily had foundered were floating here and there, while the loud and fearful moaning of the tempest increased the horrors of the scene.

After five days of rapid sailing, the Alexander, with a few more ships, arrived at Plymouth. The remainder of the convoy took refuge in various harbours, along the coast, and by the 5th of January they were all safe at anchor, in the several ports which with so much difficulty they made. On the 15th we sailed for Falmouth, when permission was granted for the men to land in detachments, in order that they might stretch their limbs after their long confinement*.

The weather having at length become settled, the fleet again got under way, and, with a fine steady breeze from the East, soon cleared the Lizard. Steering towards our friend old Biscay, of blustrous memory, we speedily lost

* Before our departure from Falmouth our society was unfortunately deprived of Captain Bentley, who remained to effect an exchange. He was, for a considerable time, staff Captain at Chatham, and was promoted to the rank of Major, when he was appointed to the 16th foot, stationed at Ceylon. He died soon after this, justly lamented by all his friends and comrades.

Bentley was succeeded, in the Alexander, by Captain Richard Stowe, a weather-beaten veteran, upon whose visage time, and hard service, had imprinted numerous deep and indelible marks.

Stowe exchanged into a West India regiment, before we landed in Portugal, and was taken off by fever in one of the Leeward Islands.

sight of the shores of Britain; but in a state of circumstances far more auspicious than those under which we first commenced our unfortunate career.

After a prosperous and very delightful voyage of seventeen days, during which we had favourable and pleasant weather, we came to anchor in the Bay of Gibraltar, when the troops were disembarked, and occupied the barracks at Europa point, on the southern extremity of the fortress.

The transport containing the flank companies and head quarters, under Colonel Walker, had missed the convoy in the heavy gales of January, and bore away to the Southward. After being driven about the Mediterranean for some weeks, it was compelled to put into the harbour of Messina, where it continued till intelligence was received of our arrival at the rock. In a little time it joined us, and the regiment was again re-assembled, and prepared for any service.

During our brief sojourn in this extraordinary place, which is too well known to need any description here, we found many things to interest us after the monotony of a voyage. The great number of strange and curious looking personages, who figured in the streets, with their varied, many-coloured, and grotesque costumes, made the town appear as if there was a carnival or masquerade going forward, and produced a very gay and ludicrous effect. There is, however, a heavy drawback to the mirth which this motley population is calculated to excite. The close suffocating atmosphere, the filthy state of the houses, and other local circumstances, promote the reception of those unwelcome visitors, plague, cholera, and yellow fever; which are still further encouraged, if not engendered, by the uncleanly habits, and abominable customs of the Turks, Jews, and other outlandish residents of the town.

The Library, containing a numerous and splendid collection of books in every language, forms a delightful source of amusement, as well as profitable employment, to the officers, civil and military, who may be stationed in the garrison.—Over the library is a magnificent ball-room in which at all times there is a pretty good display of the young and fair* rock scorpions, together with passing visitors, and warlike heros, who have assembled to dispel that ennui which might otherwise pervade their leisure hours.

The weather was excessively hot, the oppressive closeness of the air, being increased by the reflection, from the rock, of a burning sun. Were this not tempered by the occasional breeze, wafted from the Mediterranean, the climate would be insufferable: tormented by flies, mosquitos, and other insects, we had but little rest day or night, and but for the constant occupation of the mind, combined with the excitement caused by the variety and novelty of all about us, our situation would have been any thing but agreeable in such a place, which it would almost require the nature of a salamander to endure; a nature not to be obtained except by the seasoning of a very long residence.

* A term applied to those who are born on the *Rock*.

Mounting guard one day at the New mole head, I was a witness of an extraordinary interview which chanced to occur. Lieut. Frederick Baron Meard, an old subaltern of the 50th, was upon the same duty, and, being the senior, he turned out the guard to receive the visiting field officer, then Major Wood, of the 32nd regiment; to his great surprise the Major recognized Meard as the same individual who, some years before, when in the West Indies, was the field officer of the day, to whom the main guard presented arms, when he, (Major Wood), commanded it, being at that period a Lieutenant in the 32nd.

To what corps Meard then belonged, I do not recollect, but his having sold out and again commenced his military career, will account for what may seem one of those strange vicissitudes to which men of the military profession are liable.—Meard exchanged, while we lay at Gibraltar, into a regiment in the West Indies, and soon after fell a victim to the effects of that baneful climate. Major Cholmondly Overend also returned from the Regiment at this place, having sold his commission, and returned to England. Overend was a Yorkshireman, advanced in years, and decidedly of the old school. Erect in stature, and well made, with a good military expression, he retained still enough to show that in his younger days, he must have been a handsome man. Whether he is now in the land of the living I am unable to say. The 50th, previous to the arrival of Colonel Walker, was under the command of Major Charles Hill; of whom, as he was our leader throughout a good part of the Peninsular War, I shall hereafter have something more to relate.

On the 13th of May, 1808, the Expedition, under the orders of Lieutenant General Sir Brent Spencer, sailed from the Bay of Gibraltar, and on the following day arrived off Cadiz, where the fleet remained till the 13th of June, from which period to the 27th of the same month, it was cruizing about between Cape St. Vincent, Ayamonte and Trafalgar point; this being the second time of its visiting the coast in that quarter. Being appointed to do duty in Captain Armstrong's Company, I embarked with that officer, together with Ensign John Atkinson, and Quarter-Master Benjamin Baxter, on board of a fine well-built transport, called the Rosina. Our voyage was passed in a dull and listless manner, solely occupied as we were, for above six weeks, in sailing along the coasts of Algarve and Andalusia, and remaining in total ignorance of our final destination.—We were becalmed for days under a broiling sun, occasionally running short of water, and fresh provisions; and our state of uncertainty, as well as hope deferred, was enough to exhaust the patience of the most enduring mortals. Whenever the wind was favourable, or that we stood in close to the land, the natives approached the ship, with boats well laden with various articles, in the welcome shape of fruit, vegetables, or fish, which they gladly disposed of at a moderate rate. These might well be called luxuries, and formed an excellent accompaniment to our salt junk, upon which we had been stall-fed so abundantly that, for some time past, we had seldom any thing else for either breakfast, dinner, or supper. Had it not been for Captain Armstrong, I know not how we should have contrived to support a mode of existence, or rather of vegetation, which was so thoroughly wearisome. Fortunately he was an amusing companion, full of drollery and comic humour, and had, moreover, a fund of good songs, so that he kept us all alive.

Hostilities between England and Spain having ceased, in consequence of the invasion of the latter country by the French, preparations were made, in the most vigorous manner, to co-operate with the Spanish and Portuguese forces; and the British troops were accordingly held in readiness to disembark on any part of the Peninsula to which they might be ordered. General Spencer's Expedition, which was now destined for immediate active service, composed a portion of that army which first obtained a footing on the shores of Portugal, and which, eventually, under the illustrious Wellington, performed such glorious achievements in the field, driving the French Eagles before them, and bearing the victorious colours of Britain from Lisbon to Toulouse.

Soon after we arrived off the road of Cadiz, the French fleet, lying at anchor under the town, was summoned to surrender to the Spanish flag. This request not being complied with, the natural result was a general attack, made by the artillery on their shipping. The enemy was resolved to maintain his quarters as long as he could fire a shot, and therefore returned the salute, with all the heavy metal he could bring to bear against the works, sending in a broadside, with such tremendous effect as to rattle the tiled roofs about their ears and otherwise deface the beauty of their buildings.

Lying so far in the offing, we could see nothing but a thick cloud of smoke, rising above the calm surface of the bay;* the exhibition going forward behind this curtain, was completely hidden from our view. The cannonade,

* While we lay off the bay, the governor, Solano, being suspected of adherence to the enemy, was barbarously murdered.

however, was audible enough, and its music sadly tantalized our seamen in the fleet, who burned to lend a hand in an affair which was so much to their taste. They had, nevertheless, quite sufficient to employ their time, having to keep a pretty sharp look out, in order to prevent the smallest craft of the adverse squadron from slipping through their fingers.

Throughout the whole of the day, a heavy fire was kept up against the French vessels by the garrison, whose long continued volleys echoed from the harbour. Compelled, at length, to strike their colours, the French surrendered to the Dons, who, sheltered by their solid masonry, had endured but trifling loss, and were entitled to no particular praise for any bravery they might have manifested behind their bulwarks.

On the 4th of July we got under way, and, sailing well up the harbour, came to anchor a short distance from the Mole head, the ships of war being moored across the entrance. The men were not permitted to land; but the Officers had leave to pass a few hours on shore every day, and within that limited space we were busy enough making a tour of inspection, prying into every street, lane, and alley, not in search of the picturesque, but of any thing else, that might lie in our way, deserving notice from inquisitive travellers.

Cadiz is delightfully situated upon an islet, separated from the main land by a narrow strait. It appeared a paradise to us, after the long imprisonment we had suffered, from the time we left Gibraltar. The citizens were highly gratified on seeing the English Officers, and used every means in their power to evince their friendship and good will, inviting us to their houses and entertaining us with liberality and kindness. In the course of a few days the transports containing the 50th were anchored near Port St. Mary's, a considerable town on the opposite shore. Here the regiment was landed, and, after remaining for one week, was again embarked. The fleet sailed on the 22nd, and we steered once more towards Cape St. Vincent. Portugal was our destination.

Before we left St. Mary's, I was removed to

Captain Coote's company, with which I went on board the Britannia, Captain Clarke. The other officers of the cabin were Major Hill, Lieut. Birchall, Ensign Atkinson, and Assistant Surgeon Coulson, who formed a pleasant, convivial party, among whom good fellowship and social harmony prevailed.

CHAPTER III.

Upon our arrival off Mondego Bay, in Portugal, we received orders to disembark at the little village of Figueras, at the mouth of the Mondego river, across which there was a dangerous surf and ground swell. The passing of this obstacle we found to be a most hazardous and difficult service. As soon as the Portuguese boats, crowded with our soldiers, reached the foaming and rapid surge, a desperate pull was made by all the rowers; when, dashing over its surface, we were launched upon the strand in a most unceremonious manner, being pitched, or rather tumbled out, more like a cargo of fish than a boat load of gentlemen warriors. Bundled out upon the sandy beach, we lay floundering, and drenched by the waves, like so many half drowned wretches, who had lately escaped from Neptune's watery domains; and were almost doubtful of our existence, as we scrambled high, though not dry, upon the shore.—After this delightful immersion, and the cold reception we had experienced, on our first appearance upon the Lusitanian stage, we moved forward, with habiliments of war effectually saturated by the briny element, and soon joined our *companions of the bath*, already on the road. Most of us had been provided with small knapsacks, holding our *kit*, together with the haversack, and canteen, slung across the shoulder; of which the two former, (including their contents,) were rendered totally unfit for service, nothing being left for consolation but the brandy, or rum; cordials which were well calculated, and by no means unnecessary, to elevate our drooping spirits.

As soon as we recovered from the effects of

our chilling ablutions, we proceeded to the ground of encampment, and, although we were in a sorry condition with regard to the outward man, the inward was sustained by a hearty determination to bear up under privations alike inevitable to all. The weather was beautifully fine; the roads, which were in general good, led through a picturesque and richly cultivated country. At the termination of each day's march, the troops were halted in the neighbourhood of wood and water. The alignement being taken up, and the arms piled in column, fires were immediately put in requisition for cooking, and in a moment the clash and clang of bill-hooks and pioneers' entrenching tools resounded on every side; while the deep woods rang again with the clamour of ten thousand tongues, and the harsh discordant sound of bugles, drums, and other noisy accompaniments, producing, on the whole, a scene not unworthy of Hogarth himself, who might have been aroused from the dead, to execute the task of depicting it, had he been entombed within the precincts of our turbulent camp.

Before daylight the army was up, and standing to their arms, formed in open column, the reveille at the same time was sounded from right to left, and echoed through the closely planted hills, giving to our enemies in the front loud intimation of our near approach, and proving that his newly arrived visitors were at all events on the alert, and came early into the field.

As we moved onward, towards Lisbon, a skirmish took place at Obidos, in which fell Lieutenant Bunbury, of the 95th Rifle corps; the first British officer who was slain in the Peninsula. This was the prelude to a more important action. Headed by General Laborde, the French took post on the heights of Roriça, where they resisted with wonderful obstinacy the combined attack of our troops. Nothing could surpass the gallantry displayed by both parties, during the assault of this strong position; and nothing but the courage of British soldiers could have forced the enemy to withdraw. On our part, the noble conduct of the old 9th and 29th regiments was conspicuous, those corps having, at the point of the bayonet, carried the whole range of hills.

It was a lovely morning, the sun rose with a splendour never witnessed in our cold latitudes, and every object seemed to smile upon our operations, at the commencement of that struggle upon which depended the slavery or freedom of a great nation.

The 50th, 45th, and 91st were brigaded together at this time, under General I. Catlin Crawford*, and these were drawn up on the road leading to Roleia. From the arrangements made, we fully expected to have had the post of honor, or rather the honor of driving the adversary from his stronghold, and waited anxiously for the order to advance; but presently, while we stood gazing about us, up comes the 29th regiment, which by their bold and decided pace gave evidence plain enough

---

* General Catlin Crawford was a tall, fine-looking man, with a fair complexion and sandy hair. He subsequently died of fever in Portugal.

General Robert Crawford, his relation, a gallant officer, was killed at Ciudad Rodrigo.

that they were selected for the service, and, cheering them with our wishes for their success, we could not avoid admiring the style in which they moved along.

The arrangements made by the French General Laborde for the defence of his position were admirably planned, and his troops behaved with great valour, contesting every inch of ground. Concealed within the close brushwood, on each side of the narrow defile, they took steady and deliberate aim, and their fire was attended with murderous effects. The 29th, however, commanded by the gallant Colonel Lake*, pressed onward, to the gorge of the pass. While they were struggling up the rugged and precipitous ascent they were exposed to a shower of balls, and, in a few minutes, the grenadier company was nearly

* Lieutenant Colonel the Honorable George Augustus Frederick Lake was the son of General Lord Lake, and rose to high military rank at an early age. He was a man of noble aspect and commanding appearance. Mounted on a milk-white charger, he led his followers on with heroic bearing.

annihilated, the chivalrous Lake falling mortally wounded at their head, while in the act of bravely encouraging his men.

The regiment still pushed forward, although with the loss of many other officers, and, forming on the summit of the eminence, was supported by the 9th; these corps, followed by others in reserve, gained possession of the heights. Beaten at all points, the enemy moved off in good order; directing his march along the sea coast by the roads to Vimeiro and Torres Vedras.

The 9th suffered considerably in this affair, and their commander, Colonel Cameron, was killed at the first onset.

The allies marched rapidly in the footsteps of the flying enemy, keeping him well in sight until they reached the hills surrounding the village of Vimeiro, where they were formed, in order to protect the debarkation of a reinforcement of men from England; which was then off the coast. These troops landed at the small town of Maceira, and were just in time for the ensuing combat, having opportimely joined before our principal adversary thought proper to shew his face.

Junot, who was general in chief, held the British in much contempt, and endeavoured to impress upon the minds of his followers, that their antagonists were a set of raw campaigners, wholly devoid of military skill. From the testimony of some deserters, who came into our lines, we learned, that the Marshal intended, before many days were over, to give us a dusting, and to brush the pipeclay out of our jackets. This cavalier determination of the Marshal afforded no small amusement to our soldiers, who promised themselves some good sport, whenever the gasconading Frenchman might be pleased to make true his words: and, not to be behindhand with him in kindness, they resolved gratefully to return the compliment, by trimming the whiskers of his gallant veterans, and powdering their mustachios, in so artist-like a manner, that the aid of a friseur should no longer be required.

In this posture things remained until the 21st of August, when both parties assembled to put in their claim to a portion of the honor and glory which were to be won on that day. By which side the largest share of those imperishable commodities was obtained, History has already recorded.

At a very early hour, on the morning of the day already mentioned, some random shots were heard in front of our piquets, which gave us intimation that the French were on the move, and we doubted not that they were about to assist our toilet in the way of brushing; in plain English, it was clear enough that they had it in contemplation to try our metal, and ascertain whether it was of a base kind or not. Under these circumstances it was quite natural that we should anticipate their wishes; and measures were accordingly taken to give them a warm reception.

Very few of us were ever in action before, and as for the smell of gunpowder, all our young hands were perfect griffins in that way. It being our initiatory battle, our minds were under no small degree of excitement. The idea of engaging in deadly strife with the soldiers of Austerlitz and Jena inspired the ambitious hero, escaped from the apron-string, with feelings of emulation well calculated to keep alive the flame of military ardour; and each, screwing his courage to the sticking place, resolved that he would be famed *for deeds of arms*, and that his name should go down to posterity under an accumulated weight of laurels.

The 43rd. (2nd battalion,) 50th, and 95th Rifle Corps were formed into a light brigade, under the command of General (now Sir Henry) Fane, and certainly I never beheld so fine a body of men; the 43rd, in particular, were a most shewy set of fellows, a healthy collection of John Bulls, hot from their own country, and equally hot for a slap at the Frenchmen. The 95th, (now the Rifle Brigade,) was commanded by Major Robert Travers*, an officer whose

---

* Major Robert Travers was promoted to be Lieutenant Colonel of the 10th Foot, and subsequently became Major General by brevet. He settled at his native place, Cork, where he died, in consequence of a fall from his horse, in 1835. He left a widow and very numerous family. One of his daughters, previously not unknown as a writer, has very recently distinguished herself by the "The MASCARENHAS; a Legend of the Portuguese in India;" an animated Romance, which displays great knowledge of character and power of description.

bravery, on all occasions, made him worthy of a place in that crack regiment. We were posted on an eminence, to the right of the village; the 50th, being the junior corps, was stationed in the centre, and consequently on the highest part of the hill. From hence, as the day was fine, and the atmosphere quite clear, we had a distinct view of all that was going forward in the front, also a tolerably good prospect in every other direction.

The country was overspread with vineyards, and, the vintage season being at hand, nothing could be more beautiful than the luxuriant foliage. Intermingled with the vines were chesnut and olive trees, while in the parts more distant, were rich and closely planted woods, forming a back-ground in good keeping with the whole of the splendid landscape.

The plot began to thicken about 8 o'clock, when a brisk firing of musketry, among the troops in advance, announced that it was high time to reinforce the piquets, which were commanded by Captain Thomas Snowe, of the 60th regiment. They were immediately strengthened by the 4th battalion company of that regiment, under Captain Coote. A sharp discharge of small arms was kept up by a cloud of French riflemen, who, gathering round under cover of the vines and cornfields, gave their fire with a degree of activity that certainly did them credit. Our men were at this time exposed in the open field, and scarcely knew from what direction the enemy were coming; but though they were nearly all young soldiers, unaccustomed to gunpowder, they behaved with a degree of steadiness worthy of their corps. Snowe in the meanwhile, with his party, which had extended to the right, was ordered to close on either flank, to support the centre, when the principal attack was made, and where the enemy, still pressing in, galled us with a peppering that was rapidly thinning the ranks, and made our situation by no means either cool or comfortable. With admirable presence of mind, Coote directed his men to take advantage of every means of cover the place afforded; and, encouraging them by his own example, they kept their ground under a galling and destructive fire, from an enemy whom they were unable to answer or even to see. At this trying moment, while in the act of cheering his little band, and urging them to behave with firmness and courage, a musket-ball struck him in the heart, and reeling back a few paces, he fell, and instantly expired. His fall did not, however, dispirit his followers, on the contrary it excited an indignant feeling, which prompted them to redouble their exertions in order to avenge his death.

Arthur Gethin Coote was a native of the south of Ireland, and had served in the 50th regiment for some years.—He was a military looking man, strong, and well built, having dark features, and sharp penetrating eyes.—He was somewhat stately in deportment, but withal a daring soldier, steady and collected in the hour of danger.

The command devolving on Lieutenant Mark Rudkin, (Captain Snowe being detached to some woods on the right,) he gave orders to retire. The piquets extending right and left immediately fell back, under a shower of bullets, from the enemy's light troops, who continued forcing on in spite of all opposition. We gave them in return the full benefit of our small shot, as we occasionally drew up, covered by the vine hedges and olive trees, that lay within our path; and in this manner, alternately firing and retreating, so as to keep the foe aloof, we gained our situation in the line.

Before twelve o'clock, the contending forces were hard at work. Dark and accumulating masses of the enemy were advancing on every side; for, resolving that this should be a decisive combat, and that he would drive us back by the road on which we came, and perhaps into the sea, Junot brought into the field every man that he could muster. Such being his determination, it is no wonder that he pushed his warriors into our very teeth. They, too, if we might judge from the coolness with which they travelled up to the muzzles of our guns, seemed to think that they had nothing whatever to do, but to cut us into mince-meat, and devour us all by way of an early dinner. To the left of Vimeiro was a chain of lofty hills, extending for a considerable way to the east-ward. Upon these the main body of the British force was arrayed, and here the contest was fought with desperation. The enemy, at last, after many a hard struggle to gain the position, was completely routed, leaving a vast number of his killed and wounded on the sides of the precipice, as well as in the hollows and ravines at its base.

The 71st Highland Light Infantry was greatly distinguished on those heights, and, with the other corps of Sir Ronald Ferguson's Brigade, charged the assailants repeatedly from the ground. They were then commanded by that fine officer, the late Sir Dennis Pack, and fully maintained the high station which they had always held in the military records of their country.

Among their wounded was poor George Clarke, their piper, who was struck by a musket ball, while cheering up his comrades in the charge. Unable to proceed, the intrepid Clarke still continued to play in animated strains the favourite national music, and with a noble spirit remained upon the spot, under a heavy fire, until, having fully accomplished the object of their mission, his regiment came back victorious to the station on the hill.*

The 50th regiment, commanded by Colonel George Townsend Walker, stood as firm as a rock, while a strong division under General Laborde continued to advance, at a rapid step, from the deep woods in our front, covered by a legion of tirailleurs, who quickened their pace as they neared our line. Walker now ordered his men to prepare for close attack, and he watched with eagle eye the favorable moment for pouncing on the enemy.

When the latter, in a compact mass, arrived sufficiently up the hill, now bristled with bayonets, the black cuffs poured in a well directed volley upon the dense array. Then, cheering loudly, and led on by its gallant chief, the whole regiment rushed forward to the charge.

* Clarke received a handsome pension, and was justly rewarded, by the Highland Society, with an appropriate silver medal.

penetrated the formidable columns, and carried all before it. The confusion into which the panic-struck Frenchmen were thrown it would be difficult to express. No longer able to withstand the British steel, Laborde and his invincibles made a headlong retreat, and never looked behind them till they reached the forest and vineyards in the rear.

As far as the eye could reach over the well planted valley, and across the open country lying beyond the forest, the fugitives were running in wild disorder, their white sheep-skin knapsacks discernible among woods far distant. There were, however, many resolute fellows, who, in retiring, took cover behind the hedgerows, saluting us with parting volleys, which did considerable execution amongst our advancing troops. At length, even this remnant of the vanquished foe, dispersed and broken in piece-meal, betook themselves to flight in every quarter of the field. The ground was thickly strewed with muskets, side arms, bayonets, accoutrements, and well-filled knapsacks, all of which had been hastily flung away as dangerous incumbrances. Several of the packs contained various articles of plunder, including plate in many shapes and forms, which they had robbed from the unfortunate Portuguese. Books of songs, romances, and other commodities of a similar kind, were scattered about in all directions; and many a tender billet-doux lay open to the profane gaze and the laughing comments of the vulgar multitude. It was amusing, after all was over, to see the strange medley of curiosities, that had, doubtless with much pains, been collected by those who lately owned them: and it was with no very nice feelings that a general inspection of the rarities took place, as soon as the defeated army had left the field.

While we were pursuing our opponents, the 20th Light Dragoons, led on by Colonel Taylor, galloped furiously past us, in order to put a finishing stroke to the business, by completing any thing that the infantry might have left undone. The horsemen, unsupported, charging the enemy with impetuosity, and rashly going too far, were involved in a difficulty of which, in their eagerness to overtake the stragglers, they had never thought; for, getting entangled among the trees and vineyards, they could do but little service, and suffered a loss of nearly half their number: their brave commander being also one of those who fell in that desperate onset.

The 43rd regiment was very much cut up, being, while employed in skirmishing, considerably exposed. I noticed at least a subdivision of their men lying killed in a deep gulley or trench, as they fell over each other, from a raking discharge of round or grape shot.

The 50th lost a great proportion of rank and file, which chiefly arose from the fire of the French light troops, while covering their column, and during their retreat. Major Charles Hill was wounded, and Captain A. G. Coote and Lieutenant I. N. Wilson were among the slain.

Upon the bleak surface of the hill, from which the regiment had charged Laborde, we bivouacked that night, and reposed our weary limbs. Although the air was cold, and our situation comfortless, yet, from extreme fatigue, we rested perhaps more soundly than the pampered alderman on his downy couch. A windmill on the summit afforded excellent quarters for the Colonel and his personal staff, while the other officers, less fortunate, crouched together, shivering outside its base.

The 50th took a standard pole and box, which were borne by a serjeant between the colours, as a trophy, during the succeeding campaigns. The French, instead of colours, display a small brass eagle, screwed to a square box of the same metal, both of which are attached to a pole or staff. This eagle is seldom exhibited in the heat of action, the staff being carried as a rallying point, in the same way, and for the same object as our banners.

The army remained on its ground during the 22nd, no measures being taken to follow up the victory that was gained. This inaction arose from Sir Harry Burrard having arrived on the field before the termination of the battle, *assumed* the command, and given orders that no further hostile movement should take place.

An armistice was now concluded, and the

French troops withdrew into Lisbon, where they lay encamped in one of the principal squares. Here they remained, by virtue of the convention of Cintra, until their final embarkation for France, accompanied by their renowned chieftain the celebrated Duke of Abrantes, and bearing away plunder enough to load a ship, and their arms to meet us at some future day, on some other battle-field.*

* It is a singular fact, that one of those regiments of Junot's army, (the 32nd Light Infantry), was engaged with the 50th at the battle of Corunna, having lost no time in returning to their old trade of basket making.

CHAPTER IV.

On the 23rd of August we commenced our march to Lisbon. As we passed through the towns and villages that lay in our course, the enthusiasm and delight evinced by the Portuguese, on seeing the English army, was unbounded. Joyful congratulations, and the exulting language of welcome, greeted us as we triumphantly moved along; and, wherever we appeared, the most cordial reception awaited us. In the soldiers of Britain they beheld friends and allies, who had come to deliver their country from the bondage of Napoleon, as well as of French subordinate tyranny and oppression. On this account, the sentiments they entertained towards us, were those of heartfelt gratitude. Those feelings were expressed with vehemence and fervour, not merely by a class or a faction, but by all ranks and ages among the people, who saluted us with loud and deafening huzzas, and with cries of "viva los Inglezes—viva, viva,—viva los officiales! viva muytos annos!" while, as we marched beneath their crowded windows, a shower of garlands, flowers, olive branches, laurels, and other harmless missiles, fell profusely upon us. Entering Lisbon from the North, the 29th, 40th, 50th, and 79th regiments halted upon an elevated space of ground, called the Campo St. Anna, where we lay undisturbed for some days. The inhabitants around entertained the officers in a most liberal manner, their anxious care being to anticipate all our wants and wishes. In the full enjoyment of the variety and amusement of the Capital our time passed rapidly away. Temptations and enticements were not wanting to allure us from the encampment, and pleasure in many shapes appeared on every side. The Opera was well attended by those who ventured at a late hour through the long narrow streets and passages; but the pedestrian found this by no means an agreeable excursion, for it is the custom here to throw out from the windows sundry fluids, not of the most savoury nature, and while the generous inmate shrieks out, "take care below!" he, at the same instant, by way of a salute, pours the contents of his pail or bucket on the pate of the luckless passenger.

The French soldiers, who occupied the Praça de Rocio, frequently insulted the British officers who were returning from the theatre. Having to pass their camp one night, in company with a friend, both of us were challenged by the sentries, who, not waiting our reply, despatched a bullet to detain us. This caused us to quicken our pace without delay, lest they should think proper to send a second messenger of the same kind, which might put an effectual stop to our further progress. With their officers, however, we were on good terms; and, while holding conversation with them, at the coffee-houses, where we met, on the subject of our late proceedings, we found them generally pleasant, intelligent men. As long as the French remained, our duties were severe; we being, on their account, kept pretty much on the alert. I must confess, however, that mounting guard upon the convent of San Vincento was not the most harassing of those duties; for the priests, and other holy characters lodged therein, were a jolly, convivial set of fellows, and regaled us handsomely upon the best of dainties, plying their guests with oceans of capital wine, which the well-fed clerigos extracted from the nethermost chambers of their venerable abode.

The intruders, bag and baggage, having finally embarked upon the Tagus, a considerable portion of the garrison of Lisbon was directed to proceed to Monte Santo, a favourable situation on the road to Cintra, and about four miles from the city. We reached that place on the 28th of September, and remained encamped there for a month. At this period, Colonel Walker being promoted, the command of our regiment devolved on Major Charles Napier, who had recently arrived from the 2nd battalion in order to relieve Major Hill, wounded at Vimeiro. The Honorable Major Stanhope and Ensign David Leslie also joined about the same time.

Orders having been issued for us to march through Portugal, for the purpose of joining General Sir John Moore, at Salamanca, the 50th regiment set out from Monte Santo on the 28th of October, at 6 o'clock in the morning. The weather was dark, with heavy rain, which fell on us most unmercifully until we got to Lisbon. We travelled by the main road to Abrantes, along the right bank of the Tagus, and, halting at Sacavem, arrived on the following day at Villa Franca. The inhabitants, on our route, were most hospitable; receiving us with a heartiness of welcome to which we had been unaccustomed in other lands. On the 30th we got into Azambuja: the road was passable enough, though in some parts rough and hilly, winding along the course of the river, which rolled between deep and thickly wooded banks. Continuing, on the 31st, through the same description of country, we entered Santarem, after a pleasant though somewhat sultry march.

The city of Santarem consists of several narrow, dark, and ill-paved streets, the houses paltry looking, and badly built, having heavy sombre windows, grated with massive iron bars, like those of their prisons. Balconies, with painted railings thrown across, relieve in some degree this melancholy aspect, but the dingy hues, added to the meanness of the streets, give the place an air of poverty and wretchedness. On our reaching the house where we were billetted, the landlord, with his worse or scolding half, ushered us into a comfortless apartment; where, in a dark corner, stood a miserable bed, which seemed to have had other occupants than human beings. On our exclaiming against this uninviting dormitory, the old crone, grumbling inwardly, conducted us to another chamber, where the domestics, and different members of the family, were busily engaged in a deadly war against the numerous population of each others heads. Starting from their interesting employment, they left us quietly in possession of the room where lay two mattresses on the unswept floor; on these we were to repose, not without the prospect of a sharp attack from the fugitives of that army with which our Portuguese hosts had been so hotly engaged.

Yet, in spite of circumstances of this kind, the life of a soldier on service, taking all things together, is the finest in the world. While he moves on, a roving adventurer, care, pain and trouble are banished from his mind; and though he is at times on short commons, and often driven to his wits' end, he but seldom repines. His sufferings give him a greater relish for the enjoyment of any good things that may be forthcoming, or any windfall that Fortune may throw in his way. Once fairly on the road, it is astonishing how rapidly the hours glide away. The formalities of parade or drill marching are now at an end, and every one indulges in that mode of perambulation which best suits him When the commanding officer is not one of your strict disciplinarians, the regimental juniors congregate together in groups, some in front, some in rear; while the men, though keeping their sections, travel in open ranks, filling the entire space of ground over which the route extends.

At the head of the column, is to be seen a host of seniors, or old hands, among whom the laugh and joke prevail; and there many a long-winded veteran inflicts upon the ears of his patient auditors a narrative as endless as the road. Ever and anon the second Major falls back, and, in order to shew his consequence and zeal, especially if a General with his staff should chance to be passing, he calls out, in a most important tone, "Gentlemen, get into your places!" "keep on the flanks!" and other friendly admonitions. As soon as he is convinced, by the approving looks of the great man with the long feather and epaulettes, that his vigilance has been duly noticed, he gallops off to his old station, and the gentlemen betake themselves again to theirs, till another appearance of the chief, when the stray sheep are again called back to the flock. By the by, I know of nothing else that these second Majors have to do, unless it be to act the part of moveable pivots for dressing up the line, (in which they are generally very fussy), or in whipping-in the young subalterns, whom they endeavour to keep in order.

The surgeon, who is often a very hearty fellow, with better things than boluses and pill boxes in his panniers—together with the adjutant, and his brethren of the staff, attract around them, in the rear, a batch of thoroughly pleasant men, who keep up such a volley of jest and drollery, as frequently to beguile the weariness of the longest march. Thanks to their amusing powers, we have often found ourselves at the gates of the town, or on the camp ground, without being aware that we had travelled any distance.

At intervals of one or two hours, each day, the troops are halted for a few minutes' rest. Then, all, as if by magic wand, are quickly squatted, and haversack being called for, the whole of them, like hungry cormorants at their prey, are soon engaged in one grand scene of mastication. Some perform a solo on the shank-bone of a well picked ham; others display their talents on the drumstick of a half-starved fowl; while the majority gnaw their way through the skinny junk of an old tough bullock. The vultures and other birds of evil omen are, meanwhile, hovering in mid air, ready to pounce upon the remnants of the feast when we are gone.

At the well-known sound of pipes, or bugle, the warriors are again (to use a parliamentary phrase) on their legs, stretching them out with renewed vigour. Among the soldiers there is likewise much of drollery and mirth, nothing makes much difference with them—it matters not whether trumps turn up or not; whether the chance be a battle, or a good billet, they are still the same, and trudge along devoid of care. Give them their allowance, and a little rest, and they require no more. Day after day I have listened to their jokes and stories, and been highly entertained by their originality and humour.

In the 2nd division, a pack of hounds accompanied the troops, and, whenever a favourable opportunity occurred, they were let loose, and an excellent *view halloo* was frequently afforded, to the great delight of the sporting characters in our line.

The Commissary, with his long and short horned regiment, marched at a convenient distance, attended by their executioners; while the train of bullock carts, laden with provender and other stores, brings up the rear. The heavy, dull, monotonous drone, arising from the friction of the cart wheels, is heard for miles, while the jingling of the bells, with which the mules are garnished, produces a concert that rings in the head of the hearer for days and nights together, answering all the purpose of an itinerant serenade.

But we must break off from this digression; for it is time to resume our march towards Salamanca.

We quitted Santarem on the third of November, and soon got into a pleasant road, winding along the banks of the Tagus, through a dark forest of olive trees, the branches of which overhung our path, and formed a refreshing shade. Marching over the summit of a barren height, we reached the Zezere, a small but rapid stream, which here falls into the Tagus. This river we crossed by a bridge of boats, and halted at Punhete, on the opposite side, where we occupied some crazy buildings, which were deserted by the inhabitants. Through a tract by no means interesting we then held our course, on the 10th, and arrived at Neisa. The ill-fed, half-clothed, and meagre Portuguese, unused to the inundation of so many soldiers, were stupified or panic struck, flying like savage animals on our approach. The weather was harsh, and the wind, moaning through the open casements, penetrated into every hole and corner of their dwellings. Little comforted by repose, our march was still continued, until we entered a range of bleak and rugged mountains, at the base of which is situated the well-known pass of Villa Velha, which takes its name from an adjacent village, and intercepts the communication on the great road into Spain.

Here the Tagus, again opening to our view, is contracted into a very narrow space, and rushes with violence between the impending rocks; on either hand the steep and lofty precipices being cleft, as if by an earthquake, form an almost impassable barrier to the progress of an army.

A pontoon bridge had been thrown across, but this was destroyed by the French, whose troops were last upon the route, and we were therefore forced to hire three small row-boats, from the Portuguese, by which the regiment was conveyed to the opposite bank, after being long detained, owing to the rapidity of the current, impeding all our efforts to get on.

Our route traversing the boundaries of Portugal, was, in many places, overgrown with brushwood, and crossed at intervals, by rivulets. Huge stones and roots of trees lay scattered here and there. The wearied soldiers toiled with difficulty along, under the most tempestuous weather, the inclemency of which was severely felt in those Alpine regions, where the cold was so excessive as to require the hardest bodily exercise to withstand its influence. In order to keep the men alive, the band and drums were frequently put in requisition, which had a marvellous effect; and our Commander, Major Napier, occasionally ordered some well-known national quickstep, when, in a moment, as if by magic, those who were tired and jaded sprung up, endued as it were with additional life and vigour, and, giving the knapsack a cast upon the shoulder, stepped out once more with fresh spirit. The music, as we approached the towns, had the twofold purpose of pleasing the inhabitants and cheering on the troops. Even the lame and weakly, although weighed down by the heavy burthen which they carried, exerted their remaining strength to make a bold appearance. On the line of march, for many a tedious league, did the officers use every means to animate their men, by giving them an example of patient endurance under every suffering. The Field Officers and Staff alone, were allowed to ride at that time; the other ranks, although from previous habits less able than even the privates to bear fatigue, had no alternative but to trudge it with their companies from day to day.

The young recruits and drummers felt the hardship most, and often upon the journey has Major Napier given his charger to one of them, or to any poor fellow who could not well get on, while with a musket, or sometimes a brace of them, on his shoulder, he walked before the regiment. Thus, by his considerate kindness for the men, he was securing to himself that respect and estimation in which they always held him, as well as actuating them to perform their duty in a manner worthy of one who, whether in quarters or in the field, never spared himself whenever an opportunity offered to promote their comfort.

The poverty of the oppressed and ill-used natives, wherever our course lay, was lamentable; the French, according to their regular system, carried famine and desolation in their train; paying for nothing, they drew their supplies by force of arms, and their marauding foragers overran the surrounding districts, forcing the peasantry, as well as those who lived in towns, to pay the expenses of their barbarous invasion. In consequence of the ravages committed on the people, there was nothing in their markets, or their shops, " a beggarly account of empty boxes ;" and the lean and sallow proprietors were proofs sufficient of the unhappy state in which their land was placed. They were so terrified, that it was difficult to prevail on them to sell even what they could spare.—Upon demanding what we could obtain from them, the reply at all times was, " no hai nada aqui," or, " we have nothing here." Seeing us rather incredulous, and on being again requested, they would persist in the refusal, with a shrug of the shoulders, and passing the fore finger twice across the nose, crying out, " nada, nada;" but, when the finger was three times moved quickly over the nasal organ, with the scream of " nada, nada, nada," the affair was finally settled, and there was no further appeal from this hopeless gesticulation.

Even when by great good luck, there was something to be had, there was still an obstacle in the way. In those days we were often puzzled by the language, and in trying to make ourselves understood, were forced to resort to a great variety of expedients. When our broken and disjointed phrases failed, we were driven to the use of signs and hieroglyphics; suiting the action to the word, we explained our wants by distorting the limbs and body into strange figures, symbolical of the article required. Officers and men were alike in this dilemma; and fortunate was the lucky genius who could jabber, though in a most indifferent way, for he was sure to get to windward of his less favoured comrades. The market-place was a stage, upon which many a brainless youth, with much more gold upon his jacket than ever his pocket carried, shewed off his slender stock of Portuguese, and palmed himself upon the natives as a person of the utmost consequence. Others expressed their wishes in a sort of gibberish, formed out of scraps of English, German, French and Latin, but without a syllable of the language wanted. The soldiers used a most extraordinary dialect, compounded of Irish, Gaelic, and the mother tongue, interlarded with a good supply of oaths, by which to impress the subject on the head-piece of the patient countrymen, who underwent their curses, rage, and sometimes worse, when the cry of "no intendes" was uttered by them.

As to signs and gestures, they were as varied as the movements of a posture-master or even punchinello. When pork or any thing pertaining to the hog, was wanted, grunting in imitation of that animal, was the means employed. The desire for eggs was signified by cackling like a hen; was a mule or jackass required, the hands were stuck up on each side above the head, to denote the length of ears, or an awful braying was put forth, enough to call the brotherhood about the performer; tobacco or snuff was demanded by a sneeze, followed, in many cases, by a tweak upon the organ in which the filthy powder was to be deposited; and milk was procured by imitating the extraction of that useful fluid from the cow. In short, for every thing there was a corresponding signal, a code of which would have formed an excellent appendage to a soldier's kit.

We arrived at Guarda in the midst of storm and rain, half drowned and miserable. Well do I remember the bitterness of the day, while toiling up the steep ascent that led us to the gates of that old town. Seeing our deplorable trim, the owner of the dwelling where we were billetted acted with true Christian humanity; he had dry clothes in readiness, together with large wood fires, hot wine, and cordials; and, by his benevolent care, we were restored to the full enjoyment of those comforts which he so generously bestowed; I have very seldom, if ever, met with such an instance of disinterested and genuine hospitality.

We now passed the frontier of Portugal into Spain, and halted for a night at Ciudad Rodrigo. On approaching the city, we were horrified by the sight of lofty gibbets, four of which were planted on the entrances, having appended to each the quarters of some unfortunate malefactor, whose limbs were blackening in the sun. These sickening emblems of their cruelty impressed us with no very good opinion of the people with whom we were about to hold friendly intercourse; and their conduct on this night was quite in character with their gibbets. A more atrocious set of men we never had the honour of being acquainted with; and so much did they appear in favour of our enemies, that we were convinced they would gladly have delivered us into their hands, if it had been in their power to do so. An officer of the 79th unfortunately got involved in a dispute, and, while passing through one of their dark and narrow streets, was barbarously assassinated by an unknown hand. The troops being obliged to march next morning, at an early hour, it was impossible to discover by whom the murder was committed; and, indeed, we were then so circumstanced, with respect to the Spanish people, that we could not closely investigate the affair. Ample vengeance, however, fell upon this city when the French got in; and in the assault and capture of the place, in 1812, plunder and destruction was its fate: on our return to Portugal, it presented to our view a heap of burned and desolated ruins.

The part of the country through which we

now marched appeared one vast plain of immeasurable extent. The heavy rains were succeeded by a gentle fall of snow; and the surface of the ground was crisped by a light pleasant frost, rendering the highway perfectly hard, smooth, and level, and most agreeable to our pedestrian feelings.

About 2 p. m. on the 25th of November, the turrets, domes, and spires, of the justly celebrated city of Salamanca were discernable, above the sandy heights by which they are encompassed. Crossing the Tormes, by means of a long antique bridge, we ascended the street leading into the great square, the windows and balconies of which were filled with the delighted people; while the countless multitudes around gave utterance to the most sincere and warm expressions of welcome, highly gratifying to us, after the murderous reception which had been given to our troops by the treacherous renegades of Rodrigo. Well pleased to find ourselves at last, after our long and harassing journey, within the gates of this interesting and ancient seat of learning, we could not refrain from giving vent to the gladness by which we were inspired, and joined our voices with those of the Spaniards, in cheering heartily as we approached.

Having secured the billets, I proceeded, along with my friend Moore, to the house allotted for our habitation, which was situated in a narrow and rather lonely street, adjoining the walls of the great cathedral, the projecting and massive turrets of which hung with solemn majesty over our humble dwelling. The patron, who was one of the officiating ministers of this church, was a man of most important exterior, with a countenance expressive of the full enjoyment of every comfort. In this respect, however, we could not aver that he was selfish; for, upon our admittance within his holy abode, our worthy host left no means untried by which to manifest the ardour of his feelings, and the high regard in which he held the English soldiers. From his well-stored pantry he plied us with every luxury: without much bashfulness or hesitation, we helped ourselves to the dainty fare, and, joined by the generous padre, we filled out large potations of his sparkling wines, in a manner that would have done credit to the most zealous bon vivant. Our venerable divine was a true disciple of that school, of which his rotundity of figure, and rosy, shining visage, were "confirmations strong as proofs of holy writ."

In Salamanca we found every preparation going forward for the advance of the army, and Sir John Moore waiting for the division under General Hope, then on its march through the South of Portugal by the Alentejo. In the meantime, we enjoyed ourselves very much, in the variety arising from the presence of so large a portion of the troops assembled here. The officers of our regiments were no less highly gratified than we were, by the affability and kindness of the people, who exerted themselves to make our residence among them as happy as we could possibly desire.

Lieutenant Hugh Birchall, of the Light Company, discovered an old acquaintance, from his native town in Ireland, in the person of a Spanish priest: who had, a few years since, come to this place, for the purpose of finishing his classical education, and obtaining a higher polish than the bogs of his native country could afford, preparatory to his entering on the holy office. The reverend divine, who eventually became a member of the clerical establishment here, introduced us to his brothers of the cloth, who, though they treated all with hospitality, directed their attention more particularly to the Hibernians, whom, considering as *bon Christianos,* they entertained with all the warmth of brotherly affection. Father Patrick, as the Irishman was called, maintained the character of his country for the convivial virtues, and he proved an excellent cicerone to all the lions of this very respectable city.

CHAPTER V.

Lieutenant General Sir John Hope's division having arrived at head quarters, the whole of the allied forces, under Sir John Moore, marched out of Salamanca on the 12th of December, 1808. The snow was lying deep on the ground; and, although the atmosphere was clear and bracing, yet the wintry and desolate appearance of all around was rather discouraging, as we faced the northern blast, coming down most wrathfully upon us, from the wild mountains of Biscay and Navarre. After passing through Toro, and other good towns, we at length halted at Sahagun, a small place, in front of which our advanced guards were posted. Here we lay encamped until the 25th, on the morning of which day the whole army was on the move, and the memorable retreat to Corunna was commenced. The troops entered upon the high road leading into Galicia, followed by 80,000 French soldiers, commanded by the renowned conqueror, Napoleon Bonaparte, in person.

The operations of this part of the campaign have been made well known by the public records; avoiding all detail, I shall, therefore, confine myself to those circumstances that happened within my own knowledge, or that may have occurred in the regiment with which I served.

Lord William Bentinck's brigade, in the 1st division, was composed of the 4th, or King's Own, Colonel Wynch:—42nd, Royal Highlanders, Colonel Sterling:—50th, Queen's Own, Major Napier.

The division was commanded by General Sir David Baird, a man with a look of military daring, and as brave as a lion. By his presence and example, the troops, (whom he never quitted,) were encouraged to proceed with order and regularity, notwithstanding the sufferings they underwent, under the painful circumstances of a retreat; and it was not until mind and body had lost all spirit and energy, that disorder or want of discipline shewed itself among the ranks. Exposed, as they were, to the most unparalleled inclemency of weather, they submitted, without a murmur, to a continuance of hard and trying service, enough to bear down the strongest constitution. To describe minutely the whole of the privations and miseries which they encountered, would far exceed the powers of any human being: no one can possibly conceive the full extent of what the soldiers were compelled to undergo, in the course of this unfortunate campaign.

The passage of the Esla, a wide and rapid torrent, was an enterprise attended with considerable loss and danger. On arriving at the margin of the river, there seemed hardly a hope of being able to get across, with so much violence did the current roll: and, uncertain as we were of the part most fordable, it was a perilous attempt for those who undertook to make the trial. There was, however, no alternative; to the other side we were to go, at any risk, for, the enemy pressing closely at our heels, the slightest delay would have produced fatal results. We therefore dashed at it, and nobly did the men perform their duty. Agreeable as the cool, refreshing stream may be in mild regions, it was by no means a very delightful task to wade past one's middle, or rather up to the neck, through the raging waters, upon a bleak and cheerless day in December. There was no use whatever in making any preparation, or in disrobing for the bath; in fact, there was no time, but with all our harness on, we were compelled to make the best way we could in the chilling promenade. Luckily a spot was found, by which the advance was sent across, and the infantry, following their leaders, struggled along, bearing their arms and ammunition above the head. After much difficulty, plunging and buffetting the angry flood, the whole at length succeeded in gaining the opposite bank; from whence, having "shaken off the watery dew-drops," and ranged ourselves in some sort of order for another stretch, we pushed away by the main road leading into the mountains.

The advantage of lofty stature was highly conspicuous in this affair, for the man of towering height strutted above the wave, with no small pride on his extent of longitude; while the poor, insignificant fellow of Lilliputian build, looked pitifully up at his more fortunate companion, bemoaning his diminutive size, as the muddy fluid either washed his pericranium, or flowed in copious volumes down his unwilling throat. As for those ill-fated damsels, our faithful attendants through storm and sunshine, it had been far better for them that they had never left their home; for, by their desire to follow the drum, they entailed upon themselves a world of trouble, and miseries enough to drain their patience to the lowest ebb. Here I gladly record the valuable services of those poor women, who, devoted to their husbands and children, underwent a series of bitter suffering almost beyond human endurance.

Toiling with their regiments through thick and thin, they never failed in their duties, and proved, in camp as well as in quarters, the most active and persevering in giving aid and useful service, whenever it might be required. Patient under every thing, they were always at hand, foraging, cooking, and rendering all kinds of assistance; while the men, borne down by hard fatigue, were often unable to help themselves. In fact, without the labours of the fair sex, we should not have been able to get on; and I shall ever respect the heroine, who has completed the range of her accomplishments, by having served with honour a campaign or two.

By forced marches, night and day, we at last arrived at Lugo, a large town on the road to Corunna; and in its vicinity, the army was drawn up in order of battle. We fully expected, from the confident manner in which the French troops were brought into the position in our front, that an opportunity would now be afforded of giving them a warming in this cold weather. After waiting, however, for nearly two days, they declined the honour of our services; and their columns closing up, in numbers far superior to that of our force, it was deemed advisable to withdraw from the field, when there was no advantage to be gained by maintaining our ground.

In consequence of the rapid pace at which we moved, the Commissariat was altogether unavailable; and, depending on the remnant of four days provisions, our lantern jaws were getting impatient for active service; for, however briskly the nether limbs might be engaged, it was quite evident that our jaws were idle, and would never prosper by their indolence. In this matter there was no respect of persons; pockets full of cash were of no particular use, nothing was to be obtained for love or money. Desolation and its accompanying train of horrors were our companions, and General Starvation, with his two aid-de-camps, Hunger and Thirst, with all the rest of his personal staff, were constantly at our elbow.

Sauntering into Lugo one day, I chanced to drop into a crazy building, the roof of which had been torn up for fire wood. There, in a dark corner, somewhat resembling a dog kennel, and where some straw had just been scattered, I espied a group of militants, busily employed about something, but about what I could not well determine. Upon closer inspection, however, it appeared that these heroes, most of whom rejoiced in the title of Colonels or Majors, were in conclave about the discussion (not of a tactical movement), but of an ill-looking fowl, that seemed from his lanky sides as if " sharp misery had worn him to the bones," or as if he had died a natural death some length of time past.—It was nevertheless a dainty morsel to them, and they were gallantly tearing it limb from limb, and gnawing the meagre skeleton, at the time I entered. I departed from a place where the craving intruder was not a welcome guest, and joined the camp, to feed on visions of the past, and ruminate on better things to come.

The greatest suffering we endured was want of sleep. In our nocturnal wanderings, those who were exhausted and overcome with fatigue, (and few were not,) supported themselves between the men; and, each leaning on his neighbour, dozing wearily along, would every now and then waken up by a sudden bump, or push, against the knapsack of the man in front: thus, alternately bumping and dozing, we travelled with a staggering pace through the dreary and wintry road. Those who were made of weather-proof and tough materials kept their places in the ranks, while others, of more feeble frame and constitution, unable to withstand the terrible effect of cold and drifting snow, of famine and want of rest, sunk to the earth, upon the bleak and barren mountain, where they speedily perished, or fell into the hands of the enemy. Heavily burthened as the men were with ammunition, there was but a small proportion of them who were able to maintain their situation in the ranks.

Lieutenant McCarthey, of our regiment, an excellent old officer and intrepid soldier, was among those who suffered most from excessive fatigue. He kept up as long as he had the power, but being somewhat worn out by hard service, he was indifferently calculated to weather out the rough work of this retreat. Faint and half frozen, he fell in the snow, and giving himself up to despair, lay for a considerable period in an insensible condition. Meanwhile some of his companions, having missed poor Mac from his accustomed place, quickly retraced their steps, and found him almost lifeless on the cold earth. By giving him a few drops of rum, they in some degree restored him to his senses, and raising his drooping head, they helped him forward to the next halting place, from whence he struggled on to Corunna, where he was severely wounded in the subsequent battle. It was about this time that General Anstruther died, in consequence of privations and exposure to the dreadful weather.

The weather, for the greater part of our

march, was unusually desperate; the mountains, by which we were surrounded, were covered with deep snow, and over the dreary waste the wind in piercing blasts swept violently, driving the hail and sleet in our faces, so as to render it a most difficult matter to get along. At intervals, rain poured down with such tremendous force, that our open and straggling columns were compelled to halt, and close up into a solid body, in order that only the exterior of the mass might be exposed to the pelting fury of the storm. To clear away the snow from the spot on which we halted was our first employment, at the termination of each day's journey; and a most delightful frigid bedchamber was modelled out, the damp ground our couch, with the canopy of heaven for a curtain; the furniture was completed by the fragment of a rock, turning the softest side of which upwards, to make it serve for a pillow, our slumbers, during the few short moments allowed for repose, were sound though unrefreshing. Occasionally crowding in groups around a huge fire, when wood could be obtained, (which was not always the case), we gathered in without much ceremony, with our feet towards the blazing faggots, and stretched ourselves out, somewhat after the manner of wild animals, patiently awaiting the unwelcome summons that was to start us from our cold and cheerless lair.

It was truly melancholy to behold this dismal picture of the exterminating consequences of war. The ravages unavoidably committed by the troops were excessive. The weather and season of the year caused it to be almost impossible to procure timber for fuel, otherwise than by destroying the miserable hovels, that lay dispersed among the hollows and ravines of these wild regions. The frame-work of doors and windows, as well as that of the roof, were put in requisition, the extreme emergency of the case demanding such resources, without which the army must have been inevitably lost.

Sir David Baird was most indefatigable in his exertions, riding with the column, passing along both flanks,* urging on the weary troops, at the same time keeping them in their ranks, and, by his orders and presence, enforcing upon the officers the necessity of attending minutely to every point of duty. Where the roads were broken up by the rapid mountain streams, he took post near the stepping-stones, laid by former travellers across the brooks, compelling all without exception to pass on

---

* While Sir David Baird and his satellites were bustling about from one flank to another, driving every one through the water without mercy, several of the knowing hands devised sundry schemes to cross the chasm dryshod; some would take a run for it, and with a hop, step and a jump get safe past the rubicon; others, in the vain attempt, were baulked half way, and, splashing on, encountered the frigid element. But, to the men, it was the best sport imaginable, to see some mighty precise and finical dandy, who, as unwilling as a cat to wet his feet, was most cautiously picking his steps, completely discomfited by the coming up of Sir David in a rage, who, reprimanding him in no very gentle tones, would send the poor shivering exquisite to perambulate the stream, to the no small chagrin of our hero, and to the delight of the whole brigade. The equestrians and gentlemen of the staff were, in general, not over compassionate; but, chuckling up in their comfortable saddles, joined in the general outcry of merriment, and in their capacity of whippers in resumed their occupation.

through the water, however deep it might be, in order that no delay or impediment should obstruct the movements of the army.—He was equally vigilant to frustrate any attempt to plunder, and, in many cases, he made the officer stand at the door of the wine house, to stop the admission of those men, who might fall out with that intention upon the line of march. A more intrepid soldier I have never seen. Of powerful stature, with a bold stern aspect, he bore in his sunburnt countenance the indication of a mind equally strong and vigorous as his body, and wherever he was stationed, military discipline was carried on with a degree of strictness, worthy alone of such a warlike and determined man.

While going through the small town of Villa Franca, which is seated in the midst of a chain of mountains, a dépôt of clothing and provisions was thrown open, and the contents thereof flung out quickly to the troops, who, having no time to halt, were puzzled as to how those things were to be disposed of. Shoes were eagerly grasped at, the men trying them on as they hastily passed along. There was no fastidious picking and choosing here, nor were we over nice as to the shape and quality of the article; whether they were the handy-work of Hoby or of humbler origin was never enquired about. Such as they were they proved to many a boon most welcome. Yet some discomfort arose from them in several instances. Here might be seen a man pinched and tottering along, making such wry faces as though he were undergoing a course of torture; while not far from him shuffled along another, in shoes, or rather churns, that were capacious enough for the feet of the Irish giant.

It was painful to behold the anxiety of the poor fellows to get some relief to their hunger; and when the pieces of salt beef and pork were thrown to them, by the commissary from the storehouse gates, they were seized upon with the same avidity with which John Bull would pounce upon plum-pudding or fat bacon; how these delicacies were to be cooked, was a difficult question to be resolved. Speared on points of swords, or transfixed with bayonet, pike, or other weapon, the exquisite morsels of junk were borne aloft triumphant to the first halting place. Few of them, however, found their way to the end of the day's march; for the men, fearing that time would not permit the dressing of the tempting viands, pitched most of them to the crows and vultures, resorting to the more accustomed and feasible luxuries of tommy (bread) and rum. Flour was likewise doled out to them in scanty pittance; but no means of culinary operation being at hand, the pulverized allowance was scattered to the winds, the luckless warriors being left to feast upon their own melancholy thoughts, or take their dinners with Duke Humphrey.

A few of the more cunning among the oldest stagers mixed up a sort of tough consistence of this same flour, with a solution of snow in dirty water, and with the aid of a flat smooth stone, by way of table, manufactured a composition, something in form and substance not unlike a nine pound shot, and which might be converted to the same use. This bit of delicate pastry, which was called a doughboy, was sometimes crammed into the haversack for future provender, and the unfortunate genius who could not manage to bake the treasured lump, devoured it ravenously in its moist and tender state. The hard sea-biscuit, soaked in rum, was a much more agreeable article of food, and it was more convenient and more readily attained than any thing else.

During occasional halts, and when we could snatch a few moments from the hands of old father Time, we contrived to get some water boiled, and, O happy man! that could succeed in procuring a decoction of the Chinese plant: still more fortunate was he who had even a brief space allowed, to enjoy the refreshing beverage, for often, while in the act of introducing the burning fluid to our impatient mouths, the old adage of 'the cup and the lip,' was verified to our cost, the aforesaid cup with its contents being hastily thrown away, after scalding our hungry as well as angry chops; the French, in a most officious manner, choosing, like Paul Pry, to intrude at that particular period upon our tantalizing and forbidden cheer.

Passing Nogales, Constantine, and other places on the route, we traversed the mountain road that wound in zigzags along the barren sides of the precipice; the wilderness by which we were surrounded having a most dreary aspect. From the promontory between Villa Franca and the latter village the money chests were overturned, and the doubloons and dollars were scattered among the rocks, from whence they rolled into the dark abyss below, forming a precious cascade of gold and silver, enough to tantalize the craving rapacity of a Jew. Many of the wanderers from the ranks got their purses lined, and it was said, that, in the attempts to gather up the cash, some fell down the steep, and were dashed to pieces in the chasms, by which the heights were intersected.

The Paymaster's trade was, in those days, quite a sinecure; with his hands thrust into his empty pockets, he was a gentleman at large, whose pay-day was a dead letter, and whose muster-roll was getting into a very reduced compass.

It was a pitiable sight, at this period, to behold the forlorn condition of the women and the children. Those who could not get upon baggage waggons, trudged along with painful steps, scarcely able to bear up the weight by which they were encumbered. Many sank during the bitter night famished, way-worn, and in the snow, with infants at their breasts, or in their arms, and in this situation were found lifeless and frozen on the following morning. Others took refuge from the storm on the dismantled ammunition carts, that lay about the road, and, trying to get shelter there, perished with their children on this frail tenement as they crouched in groups together.

The whole exhibition was one of appalling wretchedness, that would harrow up the feelings even of those who had long been familiar with lamentable scenes. The entire *matériel* of the army became a total wreck, from which comparatively small were the numbers that escaped, and but few were able to keep up with their colours upon the line of march.

Our clothes were worn to rags, the jacket being no better than "a thing of shreds and patches," metamorphosed from red to a sort of muddy claret colour; and as for shoes, O, what a falling off was there! with sole and body in a state of separation, the partnership was about to be dissolved.—They could not be said to have held out to the last, for as they approached their end, they were something like the Irishman's brogues, that were happily supplied with holes to let the water out as fast as it rushed in, and gave our feet the advantage of an excellent portable bath. The other garments were in good keeping; unmentionables, of every shade and colour, were inexpressibly worn out, and pieced in a manner that would have qualified the wearer to perform the part of Harlequin. The whole attire was surmounted by a nondescript article, vulgarly called a cocked hat, which, glazed with a substance that had once had a polish, formed a good reservoir for rain, its angular point answering the purpose of a waterspout, while the flap hanging over the dorsal region, like that of a London coal heaver, imparted to the owner, a look of a most dubious character.

Our personal charms could not by any means be made the subject of admiration, not even the best of us could vie with Adonis on that head; on the contrary, we might have rivalled the living skeleton, and many an ambitious tyro, who at home was pampered and well fed, was now attenuated into the lathy form of a spectre, and would not on any account have presumed to offer himself as a candidate for the civic chair. Of exercise and early rising we had an abundance, and as those things are said to be conducive to health, we ought to have been the most vigorous of the human race.

To the sad deterioration of costume which I have described, there was, however, one brilliant exception. It was displayed by an officer of ours, Lieutenant *****, who entertained us much by the way in which he managed matters. In the worst of times, when the rain and wind fell desperately on us during the retreat, and all were, as I have already said, covered with mud and dirt, and drenched from head to foot, with nothing beautiful to be seen about us, this lovely youth, a *diamond* of the first *water*, the very quintessence of an exquisite, seemed on all occasions as if emerged from the limits of a bandbox. His raiment and general attire fresh from the mint, he must at least, like King Richard, have had "a score or two of tailors" to adorn his person. Whether it was that he was purified by the frequent showers, or from what other source he derived his amiable appearance, I know not, but it is certain that we were completely puzzled by the magic of his toilet; and had Beau Brummel ever ventured on the field of Mars he would have resigned his claim, as prince of dandies, to our hero. I knew of only one man in the service who could approach him, and that was a well known Captain of the 34th. ***** retired soon after from the army, and cannot fail like his prototype of old, the famous Nash, wherever he may flourish, (if in this world), to be the leader of the ton, and the observed of all observers.

Towards the beginning of January, (1809) it was reported that the shipping, for our conveyance to England, had arrived in the Bay of

Corunna, and it therefore became a matter of doubt whether or not we should have a field-day with our pursuers, before the time of embarkation. With the utmost energy that men could display, the enemy, however, anxious not to lose the opportunity of obtaining, as he imagined, a certain triumph, put forth his strength to reach the coast as early as he could, and consequently our rear guard, consisting of the Light Division, was not allowed a moment's rest. Followed by great superiority of numbers, the natural difficulty of the ground, combined with astonishing exertions, alone enabled them to check the foe. Their vigilance and valour were fully put to the proof, and never did men acquit themselves better on such an arduous duty than did these soldiers.

Whenever we gained the summit of a hill, all eyes were on the watch to catch a glimpse of the long looked out for ships. One height after another was ascended, but still nothing was in sight; before us lay, in wearisome perspective, the same tedious road, that seemed as though it were never to have an end. It was a wide, well-beaten track, the distances from Corunna being marked in leagues upon huge granite pillars, or, Hibernically speaking, *milestones.* The inscription upon them being oftentimes illegible or defaced, we asked some wandering peasant, who might perchance appear, the space we had to travel; but we could hardly ever get a correct reply, for though the stupid fellow told us that we had not more than half a league to go, we generally found it more than two leagues; sometimes the brainless oaf screamed *poquito mais* (a little bit more), this *little bit* turning out at least a league, or upwards, of very honest measure. It was provoking to be thus baffled and disappointed, but there was no remedy, and the jaded itinerants kept travelling onwards, in the same dull route. At length the long wished for Bay was spread out before us; but alas! no fleet was there! The spirits of all from the height of joy as suddenly fell below zero, and the misery of hope deferred was now to be endured. The soldiers, however, soon brightened up, when told that there would still be time sufficient to give the French a drubbing; and this idea made every man spring out with a fresh supply of ardour that carried them right through.

CHAPTER VI.

On the 12th of January the 1st brigade, under General Lord William Bentinck, marched into Corunna. Proceeding along the main street, by the harbour side, the 50th was halted in front of a large convent, near the citadel, where in a short time the regiment was quartered. After such a protracted course of hard service, and ceaseless marching, the quietness of even a temporary rest was a luxury most highly valued; although we knew not at what moment we might be called again into the field.

While we were stationed here, the great magazine of powder, situated about three miles off, was blown into the air, with such an awful explosion, that the sound thereof reached the distant mountains, and shook, as if by some volcanic agency, the buildings of the town. We were not prepared for the event, which took place at an early hour, and while a few of us were seated around our canteens at breakfast, in one of the convent rooms. Suddenly a violent concussion was felt, and then a thundering noise was heard, that made the ancient fabric reel, and tremble on its base, and rattled the tiles and shingle of the spacious roof about our ears. We were amazed, I may almost say horror-struck, beyond expression, and a number of confused ideas rapidly crossed our minds; some declared it was an earthquake, others, that the enemy's cannon were battering at the walls; no one guessed at the real cause. In a state of consternation, expecting that a second peal would annihilate our tenement, and bury us in its ruins, we made a rush for the doorway, where we met the Adjutant, who explained to us the whole affair; and this turmoil of fire and gunpowder died away in smoke.

On the 15th, our brigade marched out of Corunna, and going about two miles from the gates, was drawn up in position upon the extremity of a chain of heights, extending in a semicircular form towards the North. This movement was made in consequence of the decision of Sir John Moore to give the enemy battle; for, the transports not having come round from Vigo, (into which port they had been blown by contrary winds), he determined to make one grand effort, and maintain the honour of the British army. It would thus be seen that, however irregular his troops had been, upon a difficult march, they were well prepared to meet the foe; and that their high character for steadiness, as well as courage, would never fail when called upon in the hour of danger; proving at the same time, that in the cause of England, "every man would do his duty."

Sir John Moore himself, almost worn out by constant anxiety, arising from various unforeseen causes, was yet endued with mental force as strong as ever; and, abundant in resources, he never lost that coolness and self-possession which availed him so much. Possessing great humanity, he felt deeply for the dreadful sufferings of his men, and in his exertions to alleviate them he was unremitting. Many times have I seen him go about the lines, from one encampment to another, wrapped up in his military cloak, without parade or ostentation, in order that he might personally inspect the condition of the troops, and as far as in his power lay afford them relief, and add to their comforts.

His position, as chief of the army, was one of much difficulty; and his energies were so greatly paralysed by the interference of professing friends, and the false intelligence of his real enemies, that it appears miraculous how he ever brought the forces through. His great perseverance, intrepid spirit, and warlike talent, enabled him to overcome those trials which would have broken down another man. Let those who have calumniated his name be for ever silent, when they reflect on that devotedness of conduct, by which, in the moment of peril, he preserved untarnished the fame of Britain's sons, falling himself nobly for their glory, and by their side, in the hour of victory.

The brigade was formed on the crest of the hill, with uneven ground in front, between which and the enemy's position lay a deep and broken ravine, interspersed with vines and brushwood, and traversed in various directions by numerous enclosures and narrow lanes, inclining towards the head of the precipice.

Midway between the place where the 50th stood and the opposite hill was situated the village of Elvina, consisting of a few poor straggling hovels, with a chapel in the centre, and surrounded with fragments of rock, stone walls, hedges, and close winding passages.

The whole French army, under Marshal Soult, occupied a parallel range to that upon which ours was posted, more elevated and considerably more extensive.

The troops, being stationed in the alignement pointed out, commenced the usual operations of the camp, and were, from right to left, in high spirits at the prospect of giving the

French an airing, in return for their marked attention towards us, for the last three weeks, and by way of making some amends for all the trouble we must have caused them. For some days back, it had been perceived that immense bodies were assembling, and the heights upon which they halted were literally darkened by their increasing columns. The continual beating of their drums, (without which their men can never stir), the noisy words of command, and the din of their ammunition waggons, with the rolling of their gun-carriages, rung perpetually in our ears from the moment that we arrived upon the field. The French, on every occasion, make an excessive display, with much of loud and empty sound, and at all times, in action, they put forth such frantic and discordant yells, and raise so much useless clamour, that the report of cannon is often scarcely greater.

The morning of the 16th opened with the usual routine of duty, the same exciting work presented itself, the contending parties with eager attention observing each other's manœuvres.—The weather was cloudy; but towards noon the sun shone out, and it continued fine during the rest of this eventful day.

An extraordinary stir and commotion was noticed, about 2 P. M. in the enemy's camp, after both armies had dined. From the opposite lines, numerous light troops were seen advancing in the direction of our piquets, which had been previously reinforced, and this movement was followed by a general attack upon the entire chain of outposts.

Our soldiers, deploying into line, occupied their allotted station.—Being the junior corps, the 50th was in the centre of the brigade, flanked by the King's Own, and 42nd Highlanders; in company with such men, the Black Cuffs could not fail, and they were proud, and justly too, of being enrolled with those fine regiments.

Sir John Moore was quickly on the spot, and with the experienced mind of an old and skilful warrior, he gave the necessary orders to the several officers of his army holding command. The staff were then dispersed, and flying in all directions with those orders to the various divisions, the whole of which in a very short space of time were standing to their arms. It was about 3 o'clock when the light troops advanced in multitudes against our line; rapidly descending the hill they opened a brisk discharge from their rifles upon our piquets, that lined the enclosures throughout the wide extent of the ravine. It was very polite of the Frenchmen to allow us time to get our dinners, although it will appear that they had not finished their own repast; however, to make up for this mistake, we helped them to a desert of forced meat balls, which, composed as they were of indigestible materials, formed a considerable portion of this day's bill of fare.—As soon as matters began to wear a serious aspect, the locks and flints were examined, caps tied on, and other preparatory measures taken for the deadly strife.

For the purpose of covering his forward movements, a heavy cannonade was poured down by the enemy from a masked battery on the elevated ridge. By this plunging fire our ranks were much thinned, and the round shot, booming on every side, scattered about the splinters, sand, and stones, that fell in showers upon our heads.—Pending the operations, a general assault was made upon our left, from whence the music of artillery sounded loud and incessant.

Perceiving, by the strong fire, that a French corps was pushing through the hollows, evidently with the view of turning our right flank, Colonel Wynch, of the 4th, threw back some companies of that regiment, forming an obtuse angle with the line; which effectually prevented the enemy from making any further efforts in that quarter. While this was going on, a regiment of Guards was brought up in reserve, and posted at the rear of our brigade.

The piquets being now thrown back, from the weight of fire, our men were ordered to advance to their support. Major Napier, in front of the 50th, gave the word, cheering as he led boldly forward. Passing the enclosure, and clearing all before them in superior style, they entered the village of Elvina, which was instantly carried at the point of the bayonet, and pressing still onwards, under an awful blaze, they made for the summit of the heights. Meanwhile, the light infantry, an inflexible and stubborn band, with Captain Harrison at their head, furiously charged across the broken ground, and bearing away all opposition, took lodgment in the rocks above. The hamlet being at length surrounded, its occupants rushed pell-mell into every hole and corner they could find. A number of these heroes, having ensconsed themselves within the chapel, began to amuse themselves by firing from the windows, roof, and belfry, at the soldiers. Observing their murderous design, Captain William Clunes with cool and determined bravery marched his company to attack them, and having, with all due ceremony, introduced his grenadiers to their acquaintance, the powerful fellows would instantly have demolished the chapel, in order to eject the congregation therein assembled, had they not been hindered by their leader, who, with the greatest sang froid imaginable, took his stand by the portal of the edifice, and, grasping an Indian cane of stout dimensions, threatened destruction to the inmates, if they did not discontinue their ball practice and surrender, to a man. Astounded by the Stentor-like tone in which this *notice to quit* was uttered by the huge Northern, the garrison resolved at all hazards to evacuate the premises, and, accordingly, with a desperate rush, they sallied out amongst the flankers. Many were slain upon the spot, or taken, Clunes and his party collecting a pretty fair specimen of their afternoon's work. If the ludicrous could have been thought of at such a moment, the strange and extraordinary scene was enough to excite the mirthful faculties of a philosopher. The contrast between the tall and stalwart grenadier and the diminutive Frenchmen was truly ridiculous; and the manner in which this gigantic son of Mars turned out the warriors of Napoleon, without once drawing a sword, and while shot was flying as thick as hail, was a sight well remembered by those who were present on that day.*

* Clunes was many years in the 50th, having been present with them in all their campaigns up to this period. He

Our battalion companies fought like lions, and pouring rapidly through the village upset the kettles and cooking apparatus, which were in full work throughout the streets. The savoury stews, broths and fricassees, were put *hors de combat*, and small was the number of the meagre combatants who returned to claim a portion of the half dressed fare. Having succeeded in forcing every barrier, and cutting our way through the enemy at every point, the main body of the regiment pressed on to the higher ground; "forward, forward to the hill!" was now the cry. Clambering up the steep and craggy ascent, emboldened by the example of their officers, the soldiers were

---

was one of the finest looking grenadiers in the British army; tall in stature, muscular in frame, with a countenance expressive of the cool and determined soldier. His bravery at Corunna called forth theapprobation of the Commander-in chief, by whom he was immediately promoted to a majority in the 54th. After serving in that regiment for a considerable lapse of time, he sold out, and returned to his native country. He did not long survive, to enjoy the quiet of domestic life. His death was much regretted by the few remaining veterans of the 50th, who had been his companions in the field, and his name stands high in the records of that corps.

mowed down unmercifully by continuous volleys from the crest of the mountain, almost threatening to annihilate our ranks.

The assailants were not far distant at this time from the brow of the impending rock, which, bristling with bayonets, seemed to frown in defiance upon the enterprise. But, although the dangerous attempt to crown the eminence appeared to resemble a forlorn hope, Major Napier, with determined boldness, resolved to carry, by a coup-de-main, the enemy's strong hold; waving, therefore, his sabre in the air, he loudly called upon his men to follow.—His enthusiastic spirit had urged him on, beyond the foremost of the soldiers, when he fell, severely wounded, and, before we could approach to rescue him, he was borne off speedily to the enemy's lines.*

---

* Soult behaved in a noble and disinterested manner towards Major Napier. As soon as it was discovered that his prisoner was wounded, he ordered that he should be conveyed within the lines, and receive the attendance of the most skilful surgeon in the camp. He likewise gave directions, that he should be provided with every comfort that it was possible to obtain. To complete the measure of his liberality and kind-

About this period, the right centre, forcing through the enclosures and lanes beyond the village, was exposed to a raking fire, and in consequence was most severely handled, several officers and men being killed.—Among the former was the Honorable Major Stanhope, who received a musket ball in the chest, and expired without a struggle. He was a man of dignified appearance, reserved in his deportment, but withal a zealous officer. Having joined the regiment at the outset of this campaign, his career was brief, though splendid. The same round of musketry that caused the death of Stanhope, proved fatal to both the officers of the colours, Ensigns Moore and Stewart; the former survived but to arrive in England, the latter never spoke. They were promising young men, and much regretted by every

---

ness, he allowed the Major, as soon as he was perfectly restored to health, to return to England, on parole, in order that an exchange might be effected with a Field Officer of the French army. This act was of itself enough to stamp the character of the Marshal, and was worthy of a general, than whom one more talented or brave never fought the battles of his country.

member of the corps. Among the slain were also Lieutenant John Napper Wilson, of the Light Company.

Poor Moore, my esteemed friend and companion, had all along a presentiment of his fate; and talked of it as an event inevitably to happen in the first battle. This sad foreboding, from which I could not rally him, never for a moment preyed upon his mind, which was always cheerful and contented.*

---

* Moore died at Haslar hospital, Gosport, after lingering for several weeks. The ball having penetrated his lungs, there was no possible hope of his recovery. His father was a clergyman in the North of Ireland, who had lost other sons in the service of his country.

Ensign Stewart was a quiet and amiable lad, nephew to Colonel Stewart of the 2nd battalion. His death was instantaneous, the regimental colour, which he carried, immediately fell across his body, and was picked up by Serjeant McKie, who had scarcely delivered his charge to the officer, ordered for that purpose, when he himself received a mortal wound.

Wilson, (who was before wounded at Vimeiro,) was an Irishman, and had been some years in the regiment.

At the moment when these officers fell, we were passing, thickly crowded, through a lane enclosed with loose stone walls, and the fire, to which we were sadly exposed, raked us most unmercifully. The colours, with the officers around them, formed a conspicuous mark, against which, with deadly aim, a fatal shower of bullets was discharged. It was such hot work,

Our ammunition being expended, seventy rounds per man having been already fired, and all our efforts being unavailing against such fearful odds, orders were given for us to retire; and, on being relieved by the Guards, the troops of the 1st Brigade fell back, the shattered remnant of the 50th resuming its place upon the hill, from which it had at the outset advanced.

The remainder of the day and great part of the night was employed in preparations to embark; the huts were, however, occupied, the fires were kept burning, and every thing arranged so as to prevent the French from thinking that we intended to decamp without beat of drum.

Soon after nightfall, and when the clash of arms was no longer heard, an interment of the dead took place, and many a poor fellow, who had a few hours before been full of life and

that a man would be inclined to give himself a *shake* or two, after all was over, in order to ascertain whether his head was on his shoulders.

strength, was now deposited in his narrow bed. The remains of Major Stanhope were lowered to the grave by his brother officers and comrades, with their sashes. He had worn this day a suit of new uniform, and a pair of bright silver epaulets, in which, with his military cloak around him, upon the same hour as his lamented chief, he was consigned to an honorable tomb.

While we were engaged in the performance of this melancholy duty, the Honorable Captain Stanhope of the Guards, aid-de-camp to Sir John Moore, rode up, directed by the torch light, to the mournful group. It was the first intimation which he received of his brave relation's fate. Dismounting, and overcome with grief, he took a last farewell, and having obtained his ring, together with a lock of hair, he tore himself hastily away from the heart-rending scene.

It was about 8 o'clock when the troops moved off, in perfect silence and good order. A strong piquet was left to keep the fires alive, and watch the enemy's operations. Preparing for a renewed attack upon our army on the following day, the French camp throughout the night was in a state of tumult and noisy bustle. The outposts were not allowed much rest, being serenaded with the din of hammering up their platforms for the cannon, and sounding the note of preparation for the approaching tug of war. Little did Marshal Soult know that the bird had flown; for while he was busy in the midst of all this clamour, the British army was marching to Corunna, and by daylight was completely embarked. The soldiers left upon the hill, under the command of Captain Clunes, were withdrawn about an hour before the clear light of day, on the morning of the 17th; and taking, not reluctantly, a last farewell of the encampment, proceeded to the point of embarkation. The lowness of the tide not admitting the boats to get near to the shore, the men were compelled to wade above the middle into the water previous to entering them; hence, so far as regarded this portion of the army, Napoleon's insolent and oft repeated threats, of driving the English into the sea, were undoubtedly realized.

Missing their prey, which thus so cunningly slipped from their grasp, the French were mortified in no small degree. Fighting Jack*, for once outwitted, revenged himself by ordering his bulldogs to the water side, where, being unable to proceed further, he had nothing else to do, but "grin horribly a ghastly smile," and shew his teeth. By way of a coup-de-grace, or parting gift, however, he gave us a royal salvo, which presented to his well-tried antagonists, (who were now on board), some very striking proofs of his affection, in the very tangible shape of twenty-four pounders. But we were now beyond his reach, and he might therefore as well have saved his powder and shot, which, with all their noise, did us little injury, and only excited our laughter.

The piquets were embarked in the Mary, which was at anchor so near the beach, that

* This was the nickname given to Soult by the soldiers.

for want of something better to do in the way of a little morning sport, the Marshal made use of our old tub of a transport as a target, and practised so freely on it, with his heavy missives, that it was quite time for it to sheer off. Observing this uncivil conduct, the sea-captain, pale and terrified, with all the horror of a panic-struck man, cried out, "I'll lose my ship! I'm ruined!" and running frantic to the bows, he seized upon an axe, and cut the cable. His vessel being thus allowed to swing round, she became unmanageable, and as it was blowing a gale of wind at the time, the unfortunate Mary was driven upon the rocks. The passengers and crew were saved. The troops, who thus narrowly escaped, were received by the Thomas brig, and the 50th regiment was taken on board the Ville de Paris of 110 guns.

In the hurry of departing from the Mary, no one thought of going below deck for any of his baggage; to escape without delay from the battered vessel was the only object of our ambition; nor, indeed, could a visit to the cabin be safely attempted. Some, who were on deck with their bald pates uncovered, took flight without their beavers; thankful, as the round shots flew across the ship, to decamp with a whole skin. While we were scrambling into the boats, a ponderous box of dollars, the property of Captain Gaff, of the 76th, slipped from a sailor's hands; and as it splashed into the water, poor Gaff stood petrified with horror, and when it vanished from sight, he looked as if he would have plunged after it, to rescue the precious treasure.

On the morning of the 18th of January the fleet got under way; and, after a favourable though boisterous passage, it arrived in England on the 23rd. We were disembarked at Haslar, and marched from thence to Gosport, where we remained till the 9th of February, when we proceeded on our journey to Brabone Lees, in Kent.

CHAPTER VII.

On the 18th of February 1809, after a long and rather harassing march, the 1st Battalion of the 50th arrived at Braborne Lees in Kent, where the 2nd had been stationed for some time. Both having assembled and reunited, old friends and companions in arms meeting once more, a general scene of festivity took place; the young hands entertaining their more fortunate brethren, lately returned from the field of honour, joyous living and good cheer was the order of the day, and it might be added that conviviality was the regulation for the night.

The 68th and 85th Light Infantry being in the same barracks contributed in no small extent to those revelries, and each in succession most liberally displaying the generous hospitalities of the table, this round of dissipation was continued until a route was announced to us, for both battalions of the 50th to march forthwith; the 1st for Ramsgate, and the 2nd for the town of Ashford, four miles distant. Having obtained my Lieutenancy previous to our return, and being consequently effective in the 2nd, I joined and marched with them.

Before proceeding further I must say a word or two about those friends we left behind.—The 85th, commanded by Lieutenant Colonel Cuyler, was a very smart regiment; and the officers a gay set of light bobs, full of life and glee. I never saw a finer party of young men; longing for military enterprise, they cared not in what quarter of the world it might be offered. To see those happy fellows seated round their mess table, mingled with the 50th, their delighted guests, it would have been impossible to imagine that they were so soon to be disunited;

however so it was, and great was the pity that such was to be their lot; they were in a short time after separated, and dispersed in various directions, being removed to other regiments and other destinations. More than a quarter of a century has since elapsed, in the course of which period I have met with a few of them, others have left the stage of life or retired from the service, while but small indeed is the remnant of that gallant band, who once belonged to a Regiment which has distinguished itself in many a battle field, and than which there is not a better in the British army.

The 68th was commanded by Lieutenant Colonel Johnston. The officers, more steady, perhaps, from being more experienced, than their brother flankers, were a remarkably pleasant set of men, many of whom bore the appearance of having seen some hard service.

We found Ashford a very dull and uninteresting place, the good people of which, not being particularly fond of military gentlemen, left us very much to ourselves, to cogitate as we might in our country quarters. We made this out pretty well, however, with our regimental society; and, having also some female campaigners, we carried on the war happily enough, notwithstanding the churlish deportment of our civilized neighbours. The Ashfordians, though they looked shy upon us as a body, could, nevertheless, condescend to notice such of our young men as boasted a drop of noble blood, or were graced by the possession of some ancient name. A well-stocked purse was, moreover, a good introduction to their mahogany; and the fortunate hero, whose shoulders gloried in a *pair* of epaulets, or upon whose heels the spurs might dangle, had a most excellent chance of finding favour in their aristocratic sight. The humble subs, contented with their barrack-room parties, were perhaps gainers by the arrangement; for, although they could not boast of so much tinsel or cold display, there was among them much more social manners and generous liberality, while good fellowship and unaffected mirth presided at their less splendid though far more cheerful board. In the barracks of Ashford, our companions militant were the 91st Highlanders, and the Warwickshire Militia, both of which were in capital order for any duty; the latter in particular, commanded by Colonel S. E. Steward, was a noble body of men, exemplary alike in appearance and discipline. So that any regiment of the line might consider it an honour to receive volunteers from such a corps. The 91st, under Colonel Douglas, has always upheld the distinguished character for which these Northern warriors have been famed.

In the early part of the succeeding month of May, the second battalion received their route for Reading Street, in Kent, where we got into quarters after a few days hard marching. The temporary barracks which we occupied were situated in the centre of a highly improved country, about three miles from the small town of Tenterden. The weather being delightful at this pleasant season, and our duty not being extremely severe, the time passed in a manner quite in unison with our wishes, and without any greater degree of suffering than what occasionally arose from the hardship incident to a night campaign, upon a Bacchanalian expedition. As the invitations to the feast were but "few and far between," the dangers to be encountered on this service were by no means numerous or important. Deprived by our retired circumstances of any extensive intercourse with the "gay and lively throng," we were getting somewhat rusticated, and might in time have become very quiet and harmless animals, had we been permitted so to remain. But our retirement was much too easy a mode of existence for gentlemen of the sword, and all our dreams of luxury and peace were soon disturbed, by a sudden order from the higher powers, for several of our officers and non-commissioned officers to proceed with the utmost rapidity to the Isle of Wight, in order to join a battalion of detachments, which was then forming at Albany Barracks, and which was destined to compose a portion of the expedition under the Earl of Chatham. Being included in the number allotted for this service, I accompanied the following officers, who commenced their march for Portsmouth, on Sunday the 25th of June,

1809: Captain Henry Montgomery, Captain Edward Atkins, Lieutenant William Turner, Lieutenant Richard Jones, and Lieutenant James Thomas.

With high glee, and an elastic tone of spirits, we entered upon our journey, equipped and fitted out in a most singular manner, for, such was the speed demanded on this pressing occasion, that every kind of conveyance, inclusive of coach, caravan, gig, and fish cart, was put in requisition for the more hasty removal of our martial band. Although there was something bordering on the ludicrous in the mode of our turn out, we cut, nevertheless, a most formidable and imposing figure.

With scarcely any breathing time, we pursued our hurried course, the wonder-struck natives of the towns and hamlets through which we passed staring and gazing upon us, with open mouths, while with joyous looks we dashed along, as though his satanic majesty himself was at our heels. The officers were in and outside of coaches, as the case might be, while the serjeants, corporals and drummers, mounted on vehicles of more humble pretensions, exhibited their pikes, fusils, and other weapons, stuck out of windows, doors and various similar openings. This strange and whimsical cavalcade was not unlike a moveable battering train, or a troop of warriors in ancient times, and bore no manner of resemblance to a party of modern heroes travelling genteelly, though not leisurely, on the King's highway.

On arriving at Newport, in the Isle of Wight, we soon became acquainted with the several officers who were summoned on the same duty, and who belonged to different regiments remaining in England. The battalion of embodied detachments, which was composed of men from the dépôts of those corps on foreign service, amounted to at least a thousand bayonets, and when completed for the field was a most effective and powerful body of soldiers.—With regard to costume, it was rather motley in appearance, from the many coloured facings displayed throughout the line; and the officers wearing the plain round hat, with a small feather stuck on one side like a marine, served to render still more apparent the diversity of style and fashion exhibited in our variegated ranks.

Lieutenant Colonel the Honorable Basil Cochrane, our commandant, was a bold determined officer, and strict disciplinarian. He belonged to the 36th, in which he afterwards served in the Peninsular war, and having a natural genius for a military life, he, like his brother of nautical celebrity, was conspicuous on many occasions, during that hard fought contest.

The arrangements being concluded, our medley battalion marched to West Cowes, where it embarked, on the 15th of July, on board of the Weymouth, armed en flute, Captain Tremmer, and on the following day we sailed to Spithead, where, the troops being much crowded, some of them were removed to the Clarence Transport*. We steered for the

* The night before we sailed from Cowes, a melancholy event took place; Lieutenant Orr, of the 79th regiment, a fine spirited young man, was drowned by some accident along side the ship, as she lay at anchor.

Downs under convoy, on the 25th of the same month. On the 31st, the whole fleet set sail with a fair wind, and beautifully clear weather, standing away to the Northward, in the direction of the Dutch coast.*

---

* *The undermentioned officers served with the battalion of embodied detachments on the expedition to Walcheren.*

Commanding Lieut. Col. the Hon. Basil Cochrane, 36th regt. *dead*
Major John Wardlaw, from 64th regiment.
Major Gomm, from 6th foot.
Major Alexander Petre, from 79th regiment.
† Captain William Bains, from 6th regiment, *killed.*
Captain Thompson, from 6th regiment, *dead.*
Captain Henry Balguy, from 36th regiment,
Captain Nathaniel Farewell, from 36th regiment
Captain Chaloner, from 36th regiment.
Captain Henry Montgomery, from 50th regiment *dead.*
Captain Edward Adkin, from 50th regiment.
Captain Cooksey, from 79th regiment, *dead.*
Captain Forbes, from 78th regiment.
Captain Mc Pherson, from 78th regiment.
Lieutenant Mc Queen, from 78th regiment.
Lieutenant Munro, from 78th regiment.
Adjutant Cameron, from 78th regiment, *dead.*
Lieutenant Orr, from 79th regiment, *drowned.*
Lieutenant Turner, from 50th regiment.
Lieutenant Patterson, from 50th regiment.
Lieutenant Jones, from 50th regiment.

† Killed on his return while gallantly assisting in the defence of a Guernsey Packet, which was attacked by a French Privateer.

On the 1st of August the troops commenced their debarkation, and the battalion of detachments landed near the village of Camp Vere in the island of Walcheren, without any opposition.

The French having taken post with their main body in the strongly fortified town of Flushing, were resolved to defend the place to the last extremity; the necessary preparations were therefore made for the attack of that celebrated fortress. Being in Sir Thomas Picton's division, we were among the number of those allotted for that duty, as well as for service in the trenches, we marched accordingly to the ground laid out for us before the works.

Lieutenant Thomas, from 50th regiment.
Ensign Bair, from 33rd regiment.
Ensign Buck, from 33rd regiment.
Lieutenant Tarleton, from 6th regiment.
Lieutenant Addison, from 6th regiment.
Lieutenant Jennings, from 6th regiment.
Lieutenant Pinkney, from 30th regiment.
Lieutenant Bone, from 26th regiment.
Ensign Tunstal, from 30th regiment.
Ensign Finlayson, from 22nd regiment.
Ensign Clarke, from 22nd regiment.
Ensign Beauclerk, from 33rd regiment.

Constant occupation having rendered it impossible to keep a journal of the siege, and having no dependence upon memory, which in general proves a treacherous friend, I must abstain from any detail, and confine my remarks to a mere outline of those affairs in which our regiment was more immediately concerned. I may, however, be allowed briefly to remark, that the stirring events of this brief campaign were productive of wonderful excitement among us; and that the bombardment of the citadel and town, and the incidents that occurred on the night preceding the surrender, were of such awful grandeur as to baffle the most descriptive powers.

On the morning after its fall, Flushing presented a thoroughly ruinous and desolate appearance, from the terrible effects of shot, shells and Congreve rockets. Almost every building had experienced their destructive power. Those which stood on ground a little raised, or high above the ramparts, together with the public edifices and towers of the churches, were completely demolished. A great portion of the town was reduced to ashes by the conflagrations arising from the flaming rockets, which, penetrating whatever they came in contact with, carried fire and ruin in their train. The wretched and despairing inhabitants, forced by the ceaseless cannonade to take refuge in their subterraneous chambers, were even there exposed to the falling shells; for these, and other projectiles, descending with amazing velocity, and piercing every floor, finished their career by an explosion, no less fatal to the building than to the unfortunate people it contained. It was a fearful and melancholy sight, to contemplate the scene, and was well calculated to fill the mind with sentiments of a most depressing nature. The shattered and riddled dwellings, apparently reeling on their base, and cast nearly off their perpendicular, seemed almost ready to come down with a tremendous crash.

The half burnt and dilapidated remains of the more important fabricks, scorched by the fire, and blackened with smoke, lay heaped in dusky and spectral masses, truly monumental of their direful fate. The deserted and gloomy streets, lanes, and alleys, were overspread with the fragments of the battered walls, accumulated rubbish, and dead bodies. The stagnant, foul and muddy canals, (by which the place is intersected), were covered with dark weeds, and on them floated the putrid remains of various animals, tainting with their pernicious odour the overheated and oppressive atmosphere. At every step we encountered the haggard, woebegone and famished aspect of starving creatures, emerging from their dreary cells, or thinly scattered here and there, whose funereal countenances might have led one to fancy that they had lately escaped from the cold and cheerless tomb. These horrible sights, with many more such, enough to harrow up the soul, glared around us on all sides, throughout the limits of this unhappy place, upon which misfortune may well be said to have set her seal.

The troops of the besieging army were drawn up, while the French garrison passing in review, marched out with the honours of war. This ceremony being ended, and the enemy having evacuated the fortress, we entered the gates, and took up our abode in the miserable and comfortless quarters allotted for our reception.

The heat of the weather was suffocating: and quite sufficient of itself to produce the sickness which broke out among our soldiers. Indeed the causes already alluded to in a little time induced a fever, or something bearing more resemblance to a plague, which led to a scene of dismay and horror, far exceeding that in which the besieged had been involved. Contagion and disease, with all their attendant woes, quickly spread their baneful influence throghout our ranks. The poisonous exhalations, and marsh miasmata from the loathsome waters of the canals, combined with the fervid and contaminated air, generated and extended that deadly endemic, to which so many of our troops engaged in this campaign became the victims. Men and officers were attacked in the most sudden and violent manner, while on parade in good health, and were led away under the fatal illness from which they were soon released by the hand of death. So destructive were the ravages of this frightful pestilence that, before many days had elapsed, our numbers were much diminished, and scarcely enough of men could be found to perform the duties of the place. The hospitals were filled, and the convalescents were reduced to so low a state, that it was a considerable time before they were fit for any service.

Leaving a subject upon which it is painful longer to dwell, it may be observed that affairs in a short time were restored to order, and the inhabitants, who remained, having ventured from their hiding places, and resumed their dwellings, and usual occupations, endeavoured as far as in their power to extend their kindness towards us. This was all they had to offer: and, while sympathizing with them, we could not but lament, that so great a portion of unmitigated suffering should have become their lot, but such is the fortune of war.

While our battalion was at Flushing the Officers frequently visited the town of Middleburgh, the capital of the Island, and pleasantly situated in its centre. It is a clean and very beautiful place, surrounded by gardens and richly improved pleasure grounds, among which are interspersed many handsome buildings and cottages, laid out with a degree of taste and neatness, seldom to be found beyond the boundaries of England. With regard to the town it is perfection itself, free from every nuisance; the houses are well built, the streets wide and regularly paved. Within doors, the love for ornamental work, combined with elegance, was forcibly evinced; the painting, gilding, and other embellishments, were most conspicuous, the walls being lined, either with the coloured delft tiles or, in those of a higher class, encased with damask, silk, or velvet. Pier-glasses and mirrors, with costly frames, chandeliers, and pictures, enlivened their rooms, the furniture of which corresponded well with these expensive decorations.

To heighten the smart appearance of their streets, the newly painted shops were shewn off to the best advantage; and, in those containing plate, or metal ware, the goods, polished and burnished up most highly, as they lay exposed for sale, were dazzling to the eye, as well as tempting to the purse of the admiring passenger. At that time, one of their annual fairs, continuing for a fortnight, was going on: this being the grand centre of attraction, the Dutchmen and their Frows, with the youthful damsels, were in numerous attendance, and seemed quite unconcerned, as if no calamity had happened to their principal sea-port. This circumstance furnished an additional proof of the proverbial apathy of these plodding islanders.

They have here a few most extraordinary customs, among which may be ranked the mode of fitting up their sleeping establishment. On entering my chamber, at the Hotel in Middleburgh, escorted by the fair though rotund fille de chambre, I perceived that the counterpane and blankets were absent without leave. On demanding of my rosy guide the cause of this, and explaining that, although the night was warm, I conceived this by much too cool a manner of slumbering, she replied by pointing, with an arch and significant smile, to a mountain of feathers. Then, by raising one corner of the ponderous bale, she gave me to understand that my weary limbs were to repose between two of these enormous beds; after which she departed with a heavy step, leaving me to ruminate upon the best mode of proceeding. As I did not possess any of the heat-defying qualities of the incombustible Monsieur Chabert, I chose the lesser of two evils, and decided upon occupying the outside place, on which I accordingly took up my station.

On the 7th of September the corps of detachments embarked at Flushing, and the fleet setting sail from the island of Walcheren, with a fair wind, arrived at Portsmouth on the 10th, where the troops were landed. Our battalion marched to Porchester Castle, from whence, after remaining a short time, the several drafts of which it was composed proceeded to Albany Barracks in the Isle of Wight, for the purpose of reassembling at their respective dépôts.

Having joined my regiment at Ospringe, in

Kent, I received leave of absence, and, passing the winter in the enjoyment of Irish hospitality, returned at the expiration of four months to the regiment, which was then quartered at Silver Hill barracks, in Sussex. Here I found all my old companions pleasantly situated, and spending their time in a very social and agreeable manner, while carrying on the war in their country quarters. As the hum-drum round of daily occupation in barracks admits of no variety, it would be a waste of my reader's time and patience to enter into particulars of our peace campaigns. A little excitement and change of things was, however, soon brought about, by the unexpected arrival of our 1st battalion, lately employed on Lord Chatham's expedition; which, under the command of Major Charles Hill, marched from Hastings on the 22nd of June. They were stationed here until the 10th of August, when they got the route for Lewes, from whence they departed, a second time to join the army in Spain.

The 2nd was ordered to East Bourne, where

they arrived on the 12th of November, 1810. In the temporary sheds, erected on the sandy beach near that town, we had excellent accommodation, and having, moreover, a good commandant, we had nothing whatever to complain of. The 81st regiment, under Lieutenant Col. Milling, and the Flint Rifles, were stationed here, and their officers being a jovial, pleasant set of fellows, our rooms presented many a display of merriment and glee, during the brief space of our companionship.

CHAPTER VIII.

On the 22nd of May, 1811, an order came from the Horse Guards for a detachment to join the 1st battalion, then on its march from Lisbon to the frontiers of Portugal. The following officers were of our party:—Brevet Major Moncrieff, Captain Benjamin Rowe, Captain William Henderson, Lieutenant Geo. Bartley, Lieutenant William Crofton, Ensign Alexander Hay, Assistant Surgeon Browne.

All were in high spirits at the prospect of going to the Peninsular army; and in this state of mind we embarked at Portsmouth on the

25th of the same month, on board of H. M. S. Romulus, commanded by Lord Balgonie. His Lordship was a Northern, and a fine athletic figure. He was fond of gymnastics, and joined the officers in their trips on shore, for the purpose of enjoying any exercise in that way, for which they might be inclined. Being a great cricketer, he also formed a party to engage in that active sport. With a man of this description to command the ship, it may easily be imagined that our time on board was happily spent, and I may say with truth, that we all regretted the hour of separation from the Romulus.

We put into Falmouth, on the 31st, owing to contrary winds, and the officers were permitted to go on shore, where our enjoyment was soon interrupted by a change of wind, which springing up favourably our little convoy once more unfurled their sails; and taking a farewell glance at the white cliffs of England, we soon found ourselves again buffetting the rough sea and restless waves of Biscay. After a prosperous voyage of ten days, we entered the Tagus; and on the 25th of June the troops disembarked at Lisbon. They marched from thence on the 2nd of July, on their route to the main body of the allied army.

At the end of a long and most fatiguing journey, we got into Abrantes on the 7th, where we found considerable delay in obtaining quarters. After waiting in the streets for more than two hours, under a burning sun, and starving with hunger, we were supplied with billets upon houses totally destitute of furniture, which, together with the wretched state of the inhabitants, formed but an indifferent commencement to our campaign. We halted at this town during the ensuing day, and employed our time in exploring the various bearings of the place. The houses are badly built and old-fashioned, and, on the whole, Abrantes seems altogether destitute of those comforts which, from its aspect at first sight, one might be led to expect. We resumed our march on the 9th, and, crossing the Tagus by a long wooden bridge, passed on without interruption, save by that which the forests on our way presented. The road was in general sandy, and full of stones, and as the sun got up we found the heat and dust intolerable; owing to these impediments, we did not reach our destined quarters until 12 o'clock, when we entered Garvaõ, 18 miles from Abrantes.

The French, whose progress on the north of the Tagus was marked with cruelty and desolation, did not, fortunately for the people in the Alentejo, extend their wanderings in that direction; this place, therefore, as well as many others, had escaped the ravages of an enemy so destructive, and been hitherto exempt from the miseries inflicted on a country that has become the seat of war.

Our detachment started from Garvaõ at 1 o'clock in the morning of the 10th, an early hour it must be admitted, but at this season the intensity of the heat precludes the possibility of marching at any other; we found it, besides, far more agreeable to make a moonlight journey when the air was cool and refreshing. We were in Gafete on the 9th, where I was lodged at the domicile of Louis Corteja, a wealthy farmer. The family of the worthy Don consisted of his wife, a plodding garrulous dame, and two lively daughters, together with a brace of female attendants. Serenissima Rosa, the eldest, was very pretty, but not gifted with the nimble-tongued accomplishments of her mother, on the contrary, she was rather stupid and forbidding in her manners; the other sister, Maria, although scantily furnished with beauty of form or feature, was, nevertheless, pleasing and agreeable; nature thus keeping an equal balance between them. On a hard mattress, upon a still harder floor, (both of which had long been occupied by a colony of bugs,) I endured a sleepless night, and looked out impatiently for the return of day. We were woefully tormented in this manner on our route; for the French, wherever they appeared, carried millions of the noxious vermin in their train, leaving a bountiful legacy to their successors, and thus increasing tenfold the dirt and misery of their habitations.

On the 11th we entered Portalegre. Our road, though passable, extended over a deserted region, planted thinly with chesnut and olive trees, with pines at intervals. Portalegre is large, populous and well built: although not regularly fortified, it is capable, from the strong ground in its neighbourhood, with the aid of some works on the adjacent heights, of making much resistance, and might be rendered formidable to an enemy by some degree of skill combined with labour, and by exertions that the Portuguese will never make. The approach leading through the North-west gate is extremely steep and difficult, causing to the men and baggage animals great fatigue. The remnant of an ancient wall affords no defence whatever; and the large and ruinous arched passages serve but to give some evidence of its former importance. The public buildings are numerous. The grand cathedral in the Praça de St. Paulo, is the most remarkable; not only for the splendour of its interior, but also for the magnificent style of architecture exhibited in the whole of the fabric. The houses are generally good, and similar to those of the other principal places through the country; but they have a cold and miserably unfurnished appearance within; they are, however, well calculated for a warm climate, having spacious and lofty rooms, with unglazed windows, at all times open, and their tiled floors being occasionally sprinkled with fresh water, an additional coolness is produced, acceptable to the parched and thirsty inmates.

During our stay at Portalegre I could see nothing of, and consequently could form no opinion as to the merits of, the fair damsels of the place, so closely were they all immured, so hermetically sealed up, within the dark recesses of their habitations. Thanks to the watchful eyes of the Argus-looking duennas, under whom they were held in durance vile, we were not gratified by even a hasty glance, and thus we were utterly deprived of a pleasure, which would have afforded some consolation for the miseries and fatigues endured in the course of our rough and wearisome service. These fair and bewitching prisoners (for such I must suppose them to be,) were by no means willing inhabitants of their dismal chambers; for as we afterwards learned, they left no scheme untried to outwit their ancient keepers, and making many an amorous survey from between their rusty gratings, would gladly have been emancipated by any of those heroes who paced beneath the windows, and by whom the various tricks and manœuvres of the black eyed Signoritas were not altogether unperceived.

Early on the morning of the 13th of July we marched from Portalegre, and passing through the villages of Azumar and St. Alaya, arrived on the following day at the heights of Torre de Moro, on the sides of which the 50th in brigade with the 71st and 92nd lay encamped. After unloading our mules, and making other arrangements, we found ourselves comfortably lodged in huts, composed of branches from the spreading oak, which grows luxuriantly on those hills; our bed was formed of rushes from the banks of the Caja, a limpid stream winding along the boundaries of the wood. The wigwam, although not furnished with a marble slab, possessed the convenience of a stone table, and a chair of the same durable material. In one corner, suspended from a twig, the haversack, well supplied with dry biscuit, was dangling, and in another the flask of rum or wine, while the paniers, or canteen, amply stored with sundry articles of provender with which to comfort the weary frame, completed the appurtenances of the humble shed, and were sufficient for the wants of the warrior ensconced therein. On the aforesaid bed, of low pretensions, covered by the camlet cloak or blanket, with the leathern portmanteau for a pillow, the tired campaigner enjoyed repose as soundly as though he were provided with all the "appliances and means to boot" to be found within a palace.

Having broken up from the lines of Torre de Moro, we proceeded to Elvas and Campo Mayor, on the frontiers, and from thence into the fertile district of the Alentejo, where, cantoned at Borba and Villa Viçiosa, we were ordered to remain during the extreme hot weather of this season. We arrived at Borba on the 22nd of July, and were speedily established in most excellent quarters, our men were chiefly lodged in an old Franciscan convent, and the officers billetted throughout the town. My billet was on the house of a rich 'padre,' who supplied generously all my wants.

Borba, or Villa Bourba, is a considerable place, though styled by the natives but a village, and is distant from Elvas five leagues, and one from Villa Viçiosa, where the other brigades of the 2nd division were quartered. It is situated in the midst of a fruitful and highly improved valley, and in the heart of a beautiful country, encompassed by hills, the summits and declivities of which were clothed with richly variegated and almost impenetrable woods, the scenery around being truly magnificent. In the immediate neighbourhood are splendid groves of orange, lemon and fig trees, besides numerous gardens, producing every description of the most tempting and luscious fruits, natural to this delightful climate. The simple yet healthful manner in which the inhabitants lived, was evident from the abundance of those gardens, stocked profusely as they were with all the necessaries of subsistence, which a people who exist chiefly on vegetable diet could require.

The most extensive and charming of those gardens is that of Don Juan de Almeida, who, being in the Brazils, has left the care of it to an old steward, from whom our officers had permission to ramble throughout its pleasant walks, whenever we might feel disposed that way: often have we enjoyed ourselves during the sultry hours, while perambulating those delicious grounds, beneath the verdant festoons, hanging from branch to branch, so closely interwoven that scarcely might a single ray of noonday sun penetrate the leafy canopy. At intervals, terminating the avenues, were white marble seats and alcoves, together with bowers, composed of shrubs and evergreens, while interspersed throughout this fairy land were numerous curiously wrought fountains, the cool waters of which were received into smooth and highly polished marble reservoirs. Sundry carved figures, on pedestals, representing their ancient kings, were scattered among the sylvan groves, seeming, as it were, to gaze with admiration on the beauties of nature and art by which they were surrounded. The houses of Borba are well built, and adapted in every way to repel the summer heat and winter cold; their floors are neatly tiled, and the doors and framework composed of solid oak. There are usually three or four extensive apartments, opening off each other, with a kitchen backwards. By means of large folding doors, thrown open in hot weather, a constant circulation of fresh air passes through the building. In winter, the blast is excluded from their rooms by curtains appended to the doors; and, although they have no fireplaces, the deficiency is well made up, by means of the brasseiro, a large circular cauldron well filled with burning charcoal, around which the Portuguese dames get in congress, discussing the affairs of the nation, while they enjoy the genial temperature diffused by the heated but rather suffocating embers.

Many religious buildings are to be found here; and among them the most remarkable is the Nunnery of St. Clara; a stupendous mass of masonry, affording, with its chapel and other appendages of monastic style, a good specimen of these saintly prisons. Enclosing this grave of all that is fair and lovely, is a wall above twenty feet in height, which gives the concern a fortified appearance, and renders escape impossible. The only mode of ingress is by means of a huge pair of folding doors, which in general are kept securely fastened by locks of ponderous dimensions. From the court yard the passage leads, by a long flight of stone steps, to the visiting rooms, to which strangers and friends of the imprisoned are admitted. In the centre of the thick and solid wall of this apartment is an opening about six feet square, furnished with a substantial iron grating, separating the aforesaid room from another, in which the Lady Abbess with her nuns may condescend to appear. The visitors being permitted the freedom of familiar converse, a round of chattering and gossip soon commences, the gaiety of which, by no means corresponding with vows of retirement from the world, would rather imply, on the part of the novices, a desire to participate once more in its lately forsaken joys and pleasures.

The Capuchin convent is a venerable looking pile, standing in the midst of a thick wood, near the town. Although dark and solitary with regard to aspect and situation, within its walls is collected as jolly a set of monks and friars as ever met together, who living, or rather merely existing, in a state of lazy indolence, are supported by the deluded multitude, and supplied most plentifully with an abundance of good things. On visiting this tomb of fish, flesh, and fowl, soon after my arrival here, I found that the friars had concluded their 12 o'clock repast, and were preparing to take their usual *siesta* in the galleries, while the mendicants and pauper monks, below, were feasting on the remnants of the banquet left by the reverend fathers. From a spacious vaulted chamber I descended, by a narrow passage of stone steps, into the kitchen or refectory, where presented to view were many indications of the luxurious and sensual manner in which those holy men mortify their living members. Within a fireplace of immense capacity lay the expiring embers of the fagots used in cooking their repast, and around were numerous stoves and ovens, the walls being garnished with a multitude of culinary apparatus, and other articles for household service. In the calderio, and kettles, were still the smoking remains of mutton, beef, and vegetables, together with an endless variety of savoury food, well flavoured with oil and garlick, the perfumes from which, though not by any means agreeable to me, were snuffed up by numerous hinds and paysanos, grinning with delight, as they peeped through the door on the tempting provender, while they stood in the grand hall of the convent. These half-starved varlets, together with a horde of begging friars, with ropes tied round their bodies, (that in many of them would have been more appropriate ornaments for their necks), were called into the kitchen, by an old barefooted monk, habited in a cloak and cowl, who did the duty of head cook to the fraternity. With an air of importance, and no sparing hand, he served out to them potsfull of the compound; the poor wretches received the dole in cork vessels, and made a hearty meal, devouring it ravenously, while they squatted like so many hungry Turks at the porch of the establishment.

On the first of September, 1811, we broke up from our cantonments at Borba, and commenced our march for Portalegre. Under a burning sun, and parched with thirst and heat, we arrived at Monteforte in the evening; and on the following day once more entered Portalegre, where we took up our quarters near a large open space called the Praça de Rocio. The sufferings of the men were extreme during this route, for, loaded as they were, each with three days provisions, and sixty rounds of ball cartridge, together with a well filled knapsack, they were almost overcome; and on arriving at the termination of this journey were scarcely able to proceed to their allotted billets. Many went into the hospital, and for a considerable time the regiment did not recover from the effects of that unusually long and harassing march. The officers, most of whom walked, were likewise foundered, and the sick report was for several weeks after filled with their names. Ensign Alexander Hay, a very promising young man, who had joined at Torre de Moro, with the detachment last come out, was attacked by fever, in consequence of drinking incautiously of cold water while under the influence of excessive heat, and he died in a few days, sincerely regretted by his companions and brother soldiers.

Our stay at Portalegre was unmarked by any extraordinary event. The miserable quarters in which the 50th was condemned to pass the winter months, were rather calculated to diminish our zeal for military life, while on the other hand, their attractions being so slight, our ardour to embark in some active business was rather encreased than otherwise. We had not, indeed, been exactly placed so as to encounter all the inclemency of the weather, but we had indisputably undergone a tolerably rough seasoning while stationed there. My quarters were at the house of Donna Elvira, an ancient maiden, who had counted at least fifty winters, her forbidding aspect might lead one to presume that no small portion of the murky gloom of those winters had been imparted to her visage, which frowned in a darkened scowl upon her ill-fated guest. A dilapidated hovel was the tenement of this famed sybil, and scanty indeed was the accommodation afforded within its shattered walls; like those in the suburbs of all Portuguese towns, it was fraught with poverty; and, as if to harmonize more with its dingy patrona, all the appendages contained therein were of broken, filthy, and crumbling materials.

I was introduced by the aforesaid hostess into a chamber of sadness, without the vestige of any thing in the shape of furniture to garnish its interior; with the exception of two broken chairs, and a ricketty table, as venerable as their proprietor, tottering upon three legs, gnawed into holes by vermin, hordes of which had long maintained undisturbed possession of the premises. After throwing an old colchaõ upon a floor unswept for ages, the presiding genius of the place departed slowly, muttering from her toothless jaws sundry uncouth sounds, which had very much the tone of maledictions.

CHAPTER IX.

ORDERS from Lord Wellington having arrived, General Hill was directed to proceed with his division towards Merida and Caceres, in hopes of being able to surprise and intercept a corps of the French army, under General Girard, as well as to re-open the communication between La Pena's Spanish troops and those of Castanos. The 2nd division marched accordingly, on the 22nd of October, from Portalegre and the out quarters. The 1st brigade, consisting of the 50th, 71st, and 92nd, under Major General Howard, was on the alarm post at an early hour; and by daylight we were pretty far on our route in the direction previously ordered.

When the clouds and mist had cleared away, the ancient castle of Alegrete, placed on the summit of a barren chain of mountains was discernible. To our left extended a long range of heights, in some parts clothed with wood, and in others with verdant pasture, the brightness of which gave the prospect a lively effect. The road was broken and uneven, and, in general, so bad, that our baggage animals could scarcely make their way. Towards noon the heaviest rain we had ever experienced set in, increasing as we pushed onwards against the storm, pelting most furiously, and blown into our faces through the clefts and openings of the mountain sides close to which we travelled. We were thoroughly wet to the skin, benumbed by the intense coldness of the cutting blast, and well nigh deprived of life and motion. However, supporting each other with hopes of better times, we jogged on amidst the ceaseless war of hail, wind and rain. We halted at the village of Codiceira, just within the Spanish frontier, where a few of us darted into one of the best looking habitations we could see. There, after taking up without ceremony a good position in the chimney corner, and before a blazing pile of fagots, we got rid of our well drenched garments; in exchange for which, cloaks and mantillas were supplied by the hands of a benevolent old dame, whose exertions to administer comfort to our exhausted frames deserve to be recorded in the annals of her country.

While we are enjoying the comforts of this snug place of refuge, I will take the opportunity of saying a few words as to certain persons who seemed to think that we had no title to such a luxury. The dragoons sometimes acted towards the infantry in rather a cavalier manner, and appeared to treat them as if they were quite an inferior order of beings. Whether it was because they had the honour of being a little more elevated from the ground, or that to their visage were appended the whisker and mustachio, and they talked their mother tongue in a lisping style, it would be difficult to determine. It is at all events pretty certain, that many of them, recently imported from the purlieus of St. James's, assumed a great variety of airs and graces, unbecoming in the field, however beautiful they might have seemed in Bond Street, and which the rough and dirty work of war and fighting failed to do away with. I can never forget the conduct of one of their noble sprigs, whose regiment happened to arrive at the town when we were halted. It was a poor place after a hard march, under bad weather and very heavy rain, but we were glad to obtain any sort of shelter in the wretched village. We had scarcely entered, when our ears were saluted with the noise of cavalry, coming down the street, and in a short space we had a sample of dragooning, such as it would be vain to look for even among the Cherokees.

Three or four of us were seated round the wide fireplace of a Spanish hearth, after taking off our well drenched jackets and accoutrements, and were enjoying the benefit of a fine blazing pile of fire, the very counterpart of that I have just described, and our servants were preparing for the culinary operations, when a loud hammering was heard at the door of the hovel, accompanied by the clanking of carbines, sabres, sabredashes, and other war-like appurtenances. At the same moment, in burst a tall, raw-boned trooper, (armed cap-a-pied, with a countenance well furnished with a most abundant crop, in which the crows might have built their nest.) followed by two others, carrying sundry hampers belonging to their masters. The intruder, who proved to be the officer commanding, gazed with awful stare upon the lodgers already in the house, and drawing himself up, as if, like Sampson, he were about to raise the building on his shoulders, called, or rather growled out, in the tone of an angry mastiff, while he curled the points of his black mustachios, "these quarters are not too good for a Col—o—nel of Dra—goons —eh!" and suiting the action to the word, he flung his implements of war on a table close at hand, with a degree of violence that shook our frail tenement to its base. His claims to supremacy being intimated to us, we gathered up our traps, and bundled out indignantly, looking round, with no very gracious glances, at the statue in whose possession we quietly left the premises, to go in search of another billet.

There was a want of courtesy and good feeling here, not in any way consistent with high bearing, and these, with many other traits of character, produced a jealousy between us, so that no very cordial intimacy could take place; nor was there much love wasted on either side. Engaged in one common cause, in duty on the same field together, all those ideas of superiority should have been forgotten, and those heroes with spurs of at least half a yard in length, should have packed up all their high opinions and fine notions, and sent them to the stores in England, there to be made use of at some future period. Such commodities never do for service, nor will they harmonise with camp or bivouac. They may pass current at home, where the pride of wealth, gold lace, and dress, go far to raise a man in public estimation; but lying in a wet ditch, or stretched by the side of a tree upon the ground, with a tattered cloak for covering, they are of little value. In that situation, a good blanket, and a well filled haversack, are worth all the lace, fringe, feathers, and aiguillettes in the British army.

About this time I remember an officer joined our camp from England, with a canteen profusely stocked, as well as a good kit. He was moreover a well dressed young man, apparently fresh from the hands of Dodd, of St. James's Street, equipped in garments that seemed as if they were pasted on his body, besides a grey frock coat, lined throughout with silk, and adorned with frogs and tassells in abundance.

Such a set of poor unfortunate gypsies as we were must have been doubtless held in little estimation by our hero, who viewed with scorn our dingy costume, tarnished and tattered in so vile a manner that even a Jew broker or an Irish beggarman would have scarcely picked them up. We had however each of us a good blanket, (and some had two) that was designed a double debt to pay—

> "By night a coverlet,
> A saddle cloth by day."

Johnny Newcome, well scented, had a good stock of odours and essences for service in the field; and instead of beef or rum, his hampers were amply stored with otto of roses, macassar oil, and other articles of sweet perfume. He glanced with horror at our ugly trim, but when he beheld the saddle cloth, he laughed outright, and called us, "blanket merchants."

It was then cold and wintry weather, the rain occasionally came down in torrents, so that when the night set in, we found our friendly coverlet a most timely aid. The green-horn, who was certainly one of his majesty's hard bargains, eyed us most wistfully askance, and, shivering in his stays and broadcloth, envied the old stagers while he tried to crouch from the rain and nipping air under any shelter he could find.

One of our fellows, an admirable wag, peeped out from beneath his fleecy counterpane, and observing the plight of Master Superfine, who lay ensconced behind the stump of an old tree, he hallooed, and bellowed out so that the whole camp might hear him, "Halloo, old boy! How do you like the blanket merchants now?" The field was in an uproar at the joke, and the unfortunate recruit having no desire for war's alarms, of which he had seen quite enough to damp his fiery spirit, took himself away soon after, and the Blanketeers never had the pleasure of seeing his pretty face again.

Having despatched these gentlemen, we will now pursue our march, in search of General Girard. Early in the morning, on the 23rd of October, the troops were assembled, and about day-light, it being clear and fine, we were on the road to Albuquerque. At a considerable distance, the celebrated castle appeared towering above the hills that constitute a branch of those which extend from the Sierra de Arronches, in Portugal, into the heart of Spanish Estrimadura.

Having gained the heights, we entered the town at its base by a narrow causeway, paved with large stones. Albuquerque, which gave the title of Duke to a patriot general, is a populous, and good sized place, enclosed by lofty turreted walls. Similar to others throughout the country, the houses are flatroofed, and the streets narrow, close and dirty.

Marching again on the 24th we passed through the thick woods bounding the Sierra, our route lying over a wide and level plain. It was late in the afternoon when we halted in a valley of broom, interspersed with cork and chesnut trees, beneath the spreading branches of which we took shelter for the night, and, wrapped up in warm cloaks and blankets, around huge bundles of burning cork, solaced our weary limbs after the labours of the day. The only habitation that we saw upon the desolate road, was a sort of Posada, a large tenement, standing on the brow of a steep hill, called La Caza de la Castilana. We continued during the whole of the following day, on the same line and at a late hour halted on the top of a high and bleak promontory, exposed to the rain, and all the miseries of a dismal bivouac; but so completely were we jaded, that we enjoyed good sleep without the aid of rocking; our chamber was sheltered from the northern blast by large bushes of thick broom. Travelling for the remainder of the night, we arrived on the morning of the 26th at Malpartida, a small straggling village, in the midst of barren grounds, with a most abundant crop of stones. The inhabitants appeared to be decent and well clad; the women were goodlooking, with ruddy cheeks, and the full glow of health. A number of buxom wenches, with stout rotundity of limbs, were seated at the door of their humble mansions on our approach; most of whom were employed in knitting, and seemed, by the eager glance of their keen black eyes, to enjoy the novel dress and martial bearing of our soldiers.

These fair ones were clothed in many colours, their bodies in jackets of brown cloth, and petticoats to match, of sparing length, thereby exposing to the rude and vulgar gaze of man their well formed pedestals. Those were encased in blue stockings with red clocks, and, to complete this part of their attire, well polished shoes with brass clasps were appendages of which they were not a little vain. The mantilla of blue or yellow, gracefully thrown across the shoulders, and a profusion of rich dark hair, neatly tied with various ribbons, imparted to the figure an air of peculiar liveliness and interest.

We started from Malpartida betimes on the 27th. The rain again poured down on us with violence, and throughout the day there was but little intermission. We rested in a field, near the village of San Antonio, under a most inclement and desperate night, without the means of cover, or any refuge from the weather. Fires were not permitted, lest the enemy should discover our movements, and, as it was intended to come upon them unawares, we travelled without the slightest noise, the most rigid silence being preserved in all our movements.

Before daylight we were drawn up in the neighbourhood of Arroyo del Molino. This place lies on the borders of a wide forest, extending along the base of the Sierra de Montanches, and was scarcely visible above the trees, the church-spire alone pointing out its retired and lonely situation, beneath the adjacent hills.

As the mist, by which the distant Sierra was mantled, gradually withdrew, we discovered that the French troops were, at that hour, quietly enough lodged in the town. Little dreaming of the near vicinity of such unwelcome visitors, they were in the full enjoyment of their slumbers; and, as they had made no arrangement to guard against surprise, our unlooked for arrival threw them into the utmost consternation.

The 1st brigade halted on some rising ground, on the road leading to the village, into which the 71st Light Infantry was promptly despatched to pay their respects, as well as to assist Monsieur in the adjustment of his toilet.

Advancing cautiously in double quick time towards the streets, without noise or sound of bugle, the light bobs soon gained possession of all the principal outlets, and although the alarm given by the enemy's pickets flew like lightning throughout the cantonments, their cavalry alone, (many of whom were pulling up their saddle girths), succeeded in making a good retreat before our men appeared. Their infantry, however, after starting from their beds, out of which they had with so little ceremony been roused, hastened with all speed towards the wood, and having extended themselves along its boundaries, a close and well directed fire was immediately opened on both sides; but the 71st in a little time pressing in rapidly, followed by the 50th and 92nd, the Frenchmen gave way in all directions. Retiring across the plain, into the depth of the forest, they flung away knapsacks, accoutrements, and other trappings, by which they were encumbered, making, as they vanished among the trees, such very good use of their legs, that we found it no easy matter to keep them within hail, or within the range of those missiles that were despatched to bring them to.

While those performances were going forward, the 3rd brigade, together with some cavalry, made a rapid flank movement on the Merida road. In consequence of this, the fugitives became hemmed in, between our troops and the mountain ridge, on the left. Making a last and desperate effort, they tried to scramble up the rugged face of the precipice, but failing in their exertions, the principal number of their veterans fell into our hands, their leader Girard, with a few of his illfated companions alone escaping across the steep and nearly impassable heights. Among the officers of rank who became prisoners was the Prince d'Aremberg. The whole of their guns, baggage, and commissariat, were left on the field.

A more complete coup-de-main was not made during the war; it was executed in a manner honourable alike to the military skill and the courage of our justly respected Chief of Division, General Hill, by whose talent and steady perseverance the brilliant achievement was planned, and carried to a successful termination, in spite of the obstacles opposed by a long march in the most inclement weather. The object of the expedition was attained in the fullest manner, and the consequences were most important to the prosperity of the succeeding campaign.

The firing on all sides having ceased, and the prisoners being collected under sufficient escort, preparatory to their final exit from the coast, our brigade proceeded in open column along the plain, on emerging from which we entered the high road to Merida, on the Guadiana, passing on to the right of the lofty Sierra. In the woods about five leagues further we encamped, and on the following day, the 29th of October, we marched into the old town of Merida, when on the 30th we halted.

This ancient town had been completely plundered, and thrown into a state of ruin and desolation, by the frequent visits of the invaders. The celebrated buildings, which for ages had stood secure from the ravages of any other hand than that of time, were now either partially dismantled, burned, or destroyed. The remains of a Roman amphitheatre, and those of the Triumphal Arch, built by the Emperor Trajan, are still, however, in good preservation, and together with the numerous vestiges of ancient structure are well deserving the attention of the antiquary.

The convents, nunneries, and other religious edifices, were converted into barracks and stables for the French army, and therefore exhibited nothing but naked walls, blackened and scorched by the fires made therein. The only place of worship that escaped the general wreck was the grand cathedral in the Plaza, which being a large unsightly pile, built without taste or uniformity, is not particularly ornamental to the town. Beyond the outskirts, are the ruins of an aqueduct, which bears upon its venerable front evidence sufficient of past respectability, and, though many centuries have rolled away since it was erected, several of its arches are still in a perfect state. On the road to Truxillo a new aqueduct has been built, which is not so light or well finished as the old one. The bridge across the Guadiana is remarkable for its great length and solidity; it has seventy-four arches, a great number of which are over a low marsh, on the banks of the river, dry in the summer months. The extent between each extremity is about eight-hundred yards. There are watch towers and seats along the battlements, and the whole structure, composed of a greyish stone, is well cemented, and seems formed to stand for as many more ages as it has already stood.

Passing through Montijo and Talavera de la Real, we arrived on the 1st of November at Campo Mayor, in Portugal, where we found good quarters and civil inhabitants. The town is fortified, and is distant three leagues from Elvas, and three from Badajos.

Campo Mayor was attacked and taken about a year before by the French, who afterwards gave it up as a situation unworthy of the garrison necessary to defend it. The houses are generally solid and well built, most of them had, however, been plundered and stripped of their interior workmanship and furniture, by their late visitors.—The streets are narrow, dirty, and ill-paved, but there are a number of respectable and well supplied shops. The market is good, and was well stocked with the abundant produce of the fertile country by which it is surrounded.

Campo Mayor was at one time one of the richest and most considerable towns in the Alentejo; but since the period at which this part of Portugal became the immediate seat of war, and the French and British troops alternately came into possession of the place, it has suffered greatly; a number of its principal houses and public buildings having been burned, and its castle, citadel, and works, much injured by both armies. There is a curious charnel house in the main street, the walls of which are composed entirely of human skulls, laid and cemented together in regular layers. The establishment has a most horrid appearance, as beheld through the bars of a small grating, and is rendered still more dismal by the pale glimmering light thrown around by a lamp suspended from the arched roof of the death-like sepulchre. The inhabitants of Campo

Mayor evinced much joy on our arrival; our late successes encouraged them to receive us with the warmest welcome, which they testified by every possible demonstration of merriment and festivity.

CHAPTER X.

We remained at Campo Mayor until the 4th of November, and from thence marched to Portalegre and Albuquerque, at which latter town we took up our quarters on the 4th of March, 1812. The intervening period, spent at our old station in Portalegre, affording no event worthy of record, I pass on to describe some matters relative to our new cantonments, particularly as those from which we had so lately departed, and where we had remained for many a dreary month, have already been noticed quite as well as they deserve.

The house in which I had the honour of being entertained with "*good dry lodging*," was built after the same plan as those usually tenanted by the lower orders, throughout this part of Spain; its interior premises consisting of a large paved space at the entrance, from which the ascent to a black-looking chamber, doing the duty of a kitchen, was by means of an irregular flight of stone steps. The dingy apartment, scantily furnished, was enlightened, or rather the darkness of it made visible, by a small casement without glass; and the premises were so badly roofed that numerous chinks through the loose and broken tiles served to render unnecessary the use of a chimney, the smoke easily finding egress through them. Fortunately the climate here is generally mild, and hence the admission of fresh air is often desirable. The ground floor, besides the hall or space already mentioned, exhibited on one side a small room, containing the sleeping apparatus, and on the other an opening, by a huge door, into the dormitory of the quadrupeds, adjacent to which were sundry holes and corners, for wood, forage, and lumber at discretion.

From Albuquerque we again departed, and after various marchings and counter-marchings, we were at last conducted to Dom Benito, where we arrived on the 22nd of March, having previously halted for a few days at Almendralejo.

Dom Benito is a large town, with a population of about five-thousand souls, and is situated in the heart of a most productive country.

I was billetted on the house of Don Diego Ramirez, whose family consisted of four fat good looking damsels, two children, and his spouse, a garrulous matron, who was very officious on this occasion. I was ushered into a handsome and well furnished chamber, where I was immediately introduced to my worthy patron, a fine jolly old don; we seated ourselves round an ample brassiero, well stored with charcoal, and were soon engaged in noisy prattle and gossip, with a fluency worthy of the most experienced adepts in the science. According to custom, sundry good-humoured wenches attended at the sideboard, pouring out the limped fluid to those who were inclined to qualify for the Temperance Society. Supper being introduced, Don Diego presided in the style of a true Major Domo. The feast consisted of a large dish of sallad and oil, with other ingredients; sweet meats in abundance supplied the place of more nutritious food; while, by way of interlude, sausages and garlick appeared, by which our olfactory nerves were agreeably regaled. These were followed by other varieties in the kickshaw line, and, in order to promote the hilarity of our carousals, wine of generous quality was freely served. The young senoras, too, were by no means shy of helping themselves to bumpers of that enlivening beverage, filled out in glasses of dimensions similar to our English tumblers. One of the damsels, named Margaritta, entertained the company with a few pleasant songs on the guitar, accompanied by the voice of her sister Francisca, while Dolores, a pretty little girl with black eyes, danced a bolero, twirling the castanets in a most bewitching style, to the delight and admiration of the joyous circle.

The Spaniards seem, at all times, to have a soul for music, and chiefly do they love the plaintive strain, as sung by the peasant girls in their enchanting manner. They are extremely fond of the Scotch bagpipe, and when the Highland corps appeared among them, all ranks and ages run to their doors and windows to listen with rapture to their piper Sandy, while he played along the streets.

Before the siege of Badajos commenced, the 2nd Division was ordered to march in the direction of that garrison, for the purpose of forming a part of the corps of observation, destined to counteract any interruption to our plans, which might be threatened by the Duke of Dalmatia, who at this time lay with his army in the neighbourhood of Seville, in Andalusia. The Divisions of Generals Hill and Graham were accordingly encamped in the woods before Talavera de la Real, three leagues from Badajos, and on the left bank of the Guadiana.

The fate of Badajos being decided, that fortress having been taken by storm, on the night of the 6th of April 1812, the 2nd Division remained in bivouac for some days, during which time, accompanied by a brother officer, I obtained permission to visit the scene of action. Passing through Talavera de la Real, we travelled all day, by the level road along the plain, and near the margin of the river. It was late before we arrived near the outworks. The evening was remarkably fine after the preceding close and sultry day; as the air was calm and serene, the most awful stillness prevailed around, undisturbed save by the occasional croaking of frogs, and a murmuring sound from the battlements, on which the footsteps of the sentinel could almost be heard. In the neighbourhood of the castle, likewise, all was still. The walls, so lately filled with combatants, frowned in dusky masses amidst the gloom. The darkness at length became so great, that it was not without some trouble that we managed to grope our way; we could make but a slow progress among the ruinous *materiel* of the siege, in consequence of our getting entangled in the dismantled batteries, ditches, trenches, gun-carriages, and many other things scattered about wherever we ventured to proceed. The solitude of the desert now reigned in a place where many a gallant fellow had so recently fallen. While we were pressing onward, we perceived a glimmering from the entrance of a tent, and finding that Lieutenant Reid, of the Engineers, was the inhabitant, we asked permission to rest under his canvass until daylight; a request which he freely granted. We pursued our course next morning through the different approaches, and with difficulty gained the drawbridge, from whence, after having taken a hasty survey of the works, as well as the ground by which the columns of assault had made their first advance, we continued over the glacis and covered way towards the main breach. Here there was sufficient to account for the dreadful slaughter that took place; for so precipitous was the ascent that, in the open day, without the slightest hinderance, the task of clambering up its front was by no means easy of performance.

The work of storming this formidable breach was gallantly attempted by the 4th and light divisions, which marched boldly up the steep, but, owing to the numerous destructive means employed against them by the enemy, few were allowed to attain the summit of the dangerous pass.

A fire, close, and exterminating, was opened upon the troops, and various other deadly missiles were showered incessantly upon the solid advancing mass, which was rendered distinctly visible by the glare of fire-balls and rockets. Bodies of the slain lay heaped about the ditch, sad and direful proofs of the fearful struggle on that well-remembered night.

Having succeeded, by means of scrambling, though not without a fall or two, in arriving at the top, our further movement was impeded by several defenses, the principal of which was a wicked looking chevaux de frise, manufactured in a skilful way, being a stout cylindrical block of timber, bristled with sharp pointed sword blades. Its extremities were mortised into the stonework of the parapet, by thick iron staples. This infernal machine was flanked by various cuts or hollows, scooped out of the revêtement, on either side, from whence well directed volleys of musketry were discharged, enfilading the whole range of approach, and proving most fatal to our men. Still further, in support of them, were deep and inpassable entrenchments, covered by loop holed walls, lined during the assault with valiant soldiers under the command of Phillippon himself. When British valour failed against such obstacles it will easily be believed that they must have been formidable indeed.

According to the statements made by those who witnessed the events that occurred on the surrender of the fortress, "the pillage and destruction that ensued, together with the riot and marauding, were such as to entail indelible disgrace upon the men who were concerned. A superficial outline is the most that could be given of the confusion that prevailed throughout the place. On all sides drunkenness and tumult appeared amidst the badly lighted streets, while soldiers, and followers of the camp, together with hordes of reckless villains, revelling in plunder, were mingled in parties, shouting and hallooing with clamourous tongues. Such of the illfated and miserable inhabitants, who had escaped the perils of the siege, were running to and fro, seeking for protection from the brutal attacks of an infuriated and savage multitude. Women and children were huddled together in groups, wildly staring, as they crouched into holes and corners, and cried loudly in despair for that assistance which it was impossible to render."*

By many winding passages we made our way to the castle, the lofty walls of which were so bravely stormed by the heroic Major Ridge of the 5th and his handful of resolute followers. Nothing short of a miracle appears to have caused the success of these men; for the rampart, which they were forced to scale by

* From an eye witness.

means of ladders much too short, was not only of tremendous height, but guarded at every point and embrasure by the most experienced veterans of the French army. The enterprise was indeed one of the most daring that ever was undertaken, and the execution of it evinced, in a remarkable manner, the coolness and bravery of those who were engaged.*

Before we departed from the place, we called to see a brother officer, Lieut. McCarthy, who, while serving as Engineer, was severely wounded in the assault.† Having enlivened the poor

* Ensign Canch, of the 5th Grenadiers, was the officer called on by Ridge to support him. Canch nobly answered the summons, and survived, but his gallant Major was slain.

† McCarthy's conduct on this occasion is recorded in the life of the late Sir Thomas Picton, who commanded the 3rd Division.

"Arrived in the ditch, the leading engineer, Lieut. McCarthy, 50th Regt. who had volunteered his services, found that the ladders had been laid upon the paling of the ditch. This brave officer finding that these palings had not yet been removed, and that they formed a considerable barrier to the advance of the men, cried out—'Down with the palings!' and immediately applying his own hands to effect this, with the assistance of a few others, he succeeded in forcing them down. Through this gap rushed Picton, followed by his men, but so fellow by our visit, we bade farewell to Badajos, and with feelings excited in no small degree by the effect of all that we had witnessed, we set forth from the gates of that fortress in rather a sorrowful tone of mind. In this wood we retraced our path along the banks of the Guadiana, and found the regiment encamped in the woods where we had left them posted.

---

thick was the fire upon this point, that death seemed inevitable."—Life of Picton, vol. ii., p. 96.

McCarthy's injury was a compound fracture of the thigh.

CHAPTER XI.

THE troops broke up from the neighbourhood of the Guadiana about the 12th of April, and, after remaining at Almendralejo and other places, without the occurrence of any thing strange or interesting, the 1st brigade of the 2nd Division arrived at Truxillo, in Spain, on the 15th of May.

Orders having been given for the brigade to march, and possess itself of the forts and Pass of Almaraz, on the Tagus, we moved off, on the 16th, to accomplish the object of the expedition. Our route was long and wearisome, extending throughout the following night. By daybreak, on the morning of the 17th, we found ourselves on the declivity of a range of steep and craggy mountains, the broken and precipitous sides of which we had been ascending for some hours before, by a narrow pathway among the rocks, all trace of its windings being almost lost amidst the wilderness of heath and broom. The night was bleak and chilling, while we were thus endeavouring to explore the passage, that lay in the direction of the river, upon the banks of which the forts were situated. In consequence of the main road being commanded by the castle of Miravete, our further progress in that line was arrested, and we proceeded, by a similar path to that which we had already travelled, into a still more wild and desolate region. With much toil and labour, we pursued our dark and lonesome way, in some parts hardly better than a sheepwalk, which did not seem to have ever been trodden by human footsteps.

The Sierra upon which we had the felicity of being perched had somewhat of an Alpine character—huge grey rocks and broken and desert hills forming throughout a dreary and inhospitable prospect. The silence of the barren waste was interrupted only by the footsteps of our troops, and the moaning sound of the wind, mingled with the screaming of sundry birds of prey, which seemed to reproach their intruders for breaking in upon their haunts, where for ages their race had lived secure from the ruthless violence of man. On this mountain ridge we remained during the 17th, getting all in readiness for the delicate piece of work which was cut out for us. Pickets and guards were thrown out upon the most commanding points, secured by whose vigilance we made all the requisite arrangements for the intended assault.

We moved off the alarm-post about nightfall on the 18th, and continued our way across the mountain ridge in a direction unmarked by any distinguishable track. It was at first intended to surprise the forts before daylight. The difficult nature of the road rendered it, however, impossible to effect this object, and we had, in consequence, no alternative but to march boldly on. Having gained the open country, we were halted under cover of some rising ground, sloping downwards to the fort. Here we waited for the rear of the column to move up, as well as for the signal to advance; and having had some breathing time, we were soon in readiness for the word. The morning was clear and pleasant, and it continued fine throughout the day.

The 50th regiment, commanded by Colonel Charles Stewart, flanked by five companies of the 71st, was ordered to storm Fort Napoleon; while the 92nd, with the remainder of the 71st, were to force the Tete du pont, and the works on the opposite banks of the river. The anxious moment at length arrived, when Lord Hill riding up to the 50th, with a coolness worthy of that distinguished man, gave orders for the assault. The word to advance was instantly hailed by the troops, while at the same time they made a rapid and steady movement to the front, and pressed onward towards the summit of the hill. The moment our caps appeared we were saluted with a volley of round shot, canister and small arms; by way of sample, or as an earnest of the reception we might expect. Nothing daunted, however, by this very rough treatment, our little columns still rushed on, though under such a galling shower, and the whole of the *glacis* was speedily covered by our men. The assault was directed on three faces of the battery; the right wing of the 50th being led on by Colonel Stewart, and the left by Major Harrison, the remaining column was commanded by Major Cother, of the 71st. The moment was critical in the extreme, for at least thirteen pieces of cannon were playing away on us, while driving along in double quick time, the grape shot rattling among our bayonets, dealt out death and destruction through our already diminished ranks, the soldiers falling in numbers right and left. "Onward! forward to the ditch!" was now called out, as the storming party rapidly advanced, and with desperate resolution all hurried, under an incessant raking fire, to the foot of the ramparts.

Having attained the ground work of the

ditch, and established a firm lodgment therein, it soon became pretty clear, that, however strong our fire-eating habits might be, we should find this spot by far too warm a berth for any very protracted residence, and we therefore commenced the most prompt and vigorous measures to escalade the walls; but, the ladders being unfortunately rather short, our efforts were for some time fruitless. By this mischance considerable havoc was occasioned; for while we were endeavouring to raise the ladders, the French grenadiers, whose great bearskin caps and whiskered faces ornamented the breastwork overhead, hurled down upon us with ruthless vengeance an infinite variety of missiles. Anxious to dislodge such ugly customers, they were in no wise particular as to what they made use of for the purpose; rolling down fragments of rock, stones of huge dimensions, round shot, glass bottles, and many other articles in the small way, so that had our pates been composed of adamantine stuff they could scarcely have resisted an *avalanche* so direful. In this situation, numbers of the men were killed or wounded, and when some of the most daring attempted to climb, they were either dispatched or tumbled over before they reached the summit.

The highest angle of the wall, on the north-east side, was furiously attacked by the 4th battalion company, whose leader, Captain Robert Chandler,* with a noble spirit, was first to ascend at this point. Waving his sword as he stood on the topmost rail of the ladder, he called on his men to push forward closely; and he then jumped on the ledge of the parapet; but while cheering on his gallant followers he was blown to atoms, his shattered remains lying extended on the slope of the rampart when the troops got in.

Whilst the left wing was thus contending against superior numbers, and knocking their

* Chandler was a a brave soldier, and a very active officer, and had served for some years as Adjutant in the 31st Regiment. It was by merit alone that he obtained his company in the 50th. He fell justly lamented by all his companions in arms. Through the humane interference of Lord Hill, a liberal pension was granted to his destitute widow and two children.

heads literally upon stone walls, the grenadiers made forcible entrance on the right of the fort; carrying all before them. The Frenchmen were soon panic-struck, and by a general and simultaneous rush made for the opposite sally port; while the troops on the other flank, taking part in the performance, were completely routed and fled across the drawbridge, to the tune of *Sauve qui peut.*

Prisoners to the amount of two hundred fell into our hands, and these fierce veterans, who had grinned so horribly upon us with their black and whiskered jaws, while they entertained us in the ditch, were now downcast and woebegone, on finding this unlooked-for termination to the drama.

Clarimont, their gallant chief, the Governor of the Fort, refused to surrender to our men, and being resolved to sell his life as dearly as he could, he placed his back against the round tower in the centre of the work, where with his sabre, he chopped away right and left, cutting down any rash desperado who ventured to approach his weapon. At length Sergeant

Checker, of the 50th Lt. Company, a fine soldier, exasperated by the stubborn obstinacy of the Frenchman, put an end to his existence with his halbert; giving to the valiant governor the fate which, in his despair, he so resolutely courted. The brave Clairmont was buried at Merida, with military honours, his remains being attended by the whole garrison, and the officers in command there.*

The Tete du pont, in like manner, fell before the bayonets of the 71st and 92nd. The Gordon Highlanders, being rather fond of introducing the cold steel upon all occasions, made free to give their opponents a specimen of their abilities in that line, and so completely did they settle the business, that we were scarcely lodged in Fort

* Checker afterwards regretted that his hand should have given the fatal blow to so gallant an enemy.

In consequence of his singular merits he became Sergeant Major of the regiment, and fell a victim to the yellow fever, in Jamaica.

Many instances of signal bravery were displayed by our troops in storming Fort Napoleon. No one was more conspicuous on this occasion than Sergeant Major Lewis, of the 50th, who was so desperately wounded that he died in a few hours after the Fort was taken.

Napoleon, when they were at the water side in full possession of their defences.

Those of the enemy who had succeeded in escaping from us and crossing, let go the ropes on the opposite bank, leaving some of the boats to float at discretion down the stream, thus cutting off their fugitives, many of whom having crowded on the bridge found their career suddenly arrested, and fell into the rapid torrent, or into the clutches of the northerns which was quite as bad.

The pontoons being quickly put to rights, the passage of the Tagus was soon accomplished, and the Scotchmen dashing forward Fort Ragusa was seized without ceremony; the luckless garrison, together with the stragglers from Fort Napoleon, literally taking French leave, fled manfully and with astonishing speed on the high road to Almaraz.*

The works were all immediately dismantled, and a train of gunpowder was laid to blow up

* The Commandant of Fort Ragusa was shot at Talavera de la Reyna.

the fort, in doing which some mismanagement arose from a cause unknown, which was productive of a fatal accident. After the fuse had been lighted, Lieut. Thril, of the German Artillery, rashly entered to examine the train, when the whole concern blew up with a most tremendous explosion, scattering the body of the unfortunate Thril in fragments to the four winds.

The forlorn hope was at first led on by Lieut W. John Hemsworth of the 50th; but that officer being severely wounded in the head on the glacis, the command was given to Lieut. Patrick Plunket, of the grenadiers, who escaped unhurt, and is now Captain in the 80th Regiment. The whole storming party may be said to have been a forlorn hope, for all were equally exposed to danger, all entering nearly at the same time. From the nature of the perilous enterprise our loss in officers and men was necessarily great. Among those who were badly wounded was Captain Robt. Fitzgerald Sandys who, after suffering for a considerable period, sunk at last a victim to its effects—Sandys was an

Irishman, and very deservedly esteemed; he had served in the Light Company during all the past campaigns, and I know of no man who was more sincerely regretted on any account.

While advancing in command of his skirmishers to cover the approach of the assailants, Captain Lewis Grant of the 71st was killed; he was an active intelligent young officer, and was spoken of very highly by his own regiment.

An affecting interview took place after the surrender of the fort, between two brothers, Laurence and Patrick Egan, who were so strongly attached that they were never content on separate duties—The eldest, Laurence, or Larry as his comrades called him, being a batman, was consequently ordered to remain in charge of the baggage of his company, on the march of the Regiment. Prompted by a noble feeling, as well as an ardent desire to be near his brother, this spirited young soldier begged so earnestly for leave to join and meet the enemy with his own companions, that he was at length permitted to do so.

The brothers behaved gallantly on the occasion, and maintained the character of Irishmen. Patrick was mortally wounded during the escalade, being one of the first to mount the ladder. Lying on the rampart in a most painful state, he lingered out for some hours. Poor Larry, in the joy of his heart on our success, ran to find out his brother, whom he soon discovered extended in the agonies of death! A more touching or affecting scene could not be witnessed, and, though it was in humble life, it was moving to the hearts of all around. Many who had long been callous to the horrors of a battle-field, and familiarized to the work of slaughter, could have wept over the deep sorrows of those truly brave and affectionate brothers. The mournful Larry never regained his spirits, and fell in one of the subsequent engagements. They were both excellent soldiers, having a good claim to this feeble record of their worth.

Thus, within a short space of forty minutes from the first onset, after a sharp contest, in which the 50th Regiment alone had a hundred and fifty officers and men put *hors de combat*, was this brilliant affair brought to a triumphant close. Of the wounded but few recovered, so severe were the injuries which they sustained. The British might justly be proud of the exploit, as it is confessed, even by French historians, that "the Forts were susceptible of a long defence."*

On the examination of the stores after the capture, we were highly pleased to find that the French had left us a valuable legacy.—Their magazines were well stocked, not only with powder and ball, but with an ample supply of provender, sufficient to rejoice the hearts of any half-starved warriors; the quality, moreover, of these materials being such as to gratify the palate of the most fastidious gourmand. To a set of fellows in our sorry plight this was no very unpleasing windfall, and

* Total British loss in the affair; *Killed*—1 Captain, 1 Lieutenant, 1 Sergeant and 30 Rank and File. *Wounded*—2 Captains, 6 Lieutenants, 4 Ensigns, 10 Sergeants, 1 Drummer and 117 Rank and File.

fighting being allowed at all times to be very hungry work, we proceeded, with appetites sharpened like our swords, on the work of demolition; the lean and starving bullocks allotted for our use being at the same time happy at the prospect of a respite from the sentence of being cut up for rations by the remorseless knife. Assembled on the esplanade, so lately the arena of our exploits, fragments of the dainty fare were dispensed with liberal hand, under the inspection of the quarter-master; and with a relish, that might have put a town councillor to the blush, we dispatched the *vivres* with as little ceremony as we had shown to the original proprietors of the same; nor were we by any means over nice, as to the mode in which our pic-nic repast was served or garnished.

Collected together in knots and parties, with the green sward for our table-cloth, forgetful of the past, and careless about the future, we feasted most sumptuously, drinking to our foes in their own generous wine, and wishing that, in future campaigns, our adventures might be terminated in an equally agreeable and fortunate manner.

CHAPTER XII.

We marched on the morning of the 20th of May, 1812, and on the 21st entered our old quarters at Truxillo. The journey was fatiguing, but, as we returned by the main road, our sufferings were not by any means so great as they were on the former occasion.

Truxillo is large and populous, and appears from the remains of its ancient buildings, castles, churches, and walls, to have once been a place of considerable note, and one of the principal towns in this part of Spain. From the hill, on which it stands, there is a commanding view, even to the mountains of Miravete. The square is spacious and uniform, the houses built in the Moorish style, their upper compartments projecting, so as to form a range of handsome piazzas underneath, where all the most respectable shops are situated. The windows above, opening to the plaza, are furnished with handsomely ornamented verandas and balconies, in front of which are appended solid iron bars. The fair Senoras occasionally display their charms at those windows, during the cooler hours, decked out in holyday robes and gaiest attire, imparting a brilliancy of effect to their balconies which it would be impossible for the most costly works of art to rival.

On the South side of the Square, the attention of the stranger is attracted to the splendid fabric, erected by the celebrated Pizarro, to commemorate the successes of his victorious arms in the Western hemisphere. It is large and solid, and of such ample dimensions that a regiment of French soldiers found space to lodge therein. On the surface of the flat roof are several marble figures, designed, it is said, to represent the Peruvian princes and warriors who submitted to the Spanish chief, in his wars against their nation. They remain, however, monumental of the barbarous cruelties exercised towards a harmless people, by a merciless tyrant, who is to this day undeservedly held up to admiration in his native country.

The principal amusements of this place are the bull-fights. Soon after our arrival there was one of those performances took place in the Plaza de Torres, to celebrate our late exploits. It was a miserable attempt to represent those exhibitions as they were in former days. Two or three unfortunate bulls were driven, or rather tormented, into a circle formed in the Square; they were then goaded by a multitude of men and boys, until the animals became almost frantic; their tormentors, throwing up hats, caps, cloaks, and sticks, while hooting and yelling forth the most abominable noises. Although this afforded *us* but little sport, it was a means of collecting a large assemblage of spectators, from all parts of the town and country, and the houses around the Square were filled; the doors and balconies, as well as the roofs, being crowded with the delighted amateurs. Numerous fair damsels were among them, dressed out in gaudy colours, attended by their duennas, to witness the barbarous entertainment.

Amidst the cries, yells, and shouting of the peasants in the ring, one of the bulls, infuriated and lashed into rage, not only by his persecutors in human form, but also by some ferocious mastiffs, would occasionally make a desperate rush in upon the mob of ruffians, and violently running down a fellow more daring than the others, would toss him up with his horns several yards in the air, to the inexpressible delight and admiration of the surrounding audience, who expressed their savage joy in loud and deafening acclamations; clapping their hands, and waving handkerchiefs and fans, by way of approbation of the inhuman spectacle. At intervals, the peasants paired off in the fandango, or bolero, with some fair sweetheart, putting themselves through the most ridiculous antics, while accompanied by the music of an old cracked guitar, or broken-winded clarionet, performed on by some wretched artist.

Truxillo must have been in the days of yore a formidable place; rendered so, not only by its elevated site, but also by the nature of its defences, and a high wall, which in ancient times completely encompassed it, of which the gates alone remain. The country immediately around it is open, presenting but little appearance of any sort of verdure, but in the direction of Almaraz, there are thick and extensive forests, of oak and other trees.

On the 12th of June we marched to Fuentes del Maestro, where I got into capital quarters, at the house of Don Diego Dias, which, though it had been occupied by French Dragoons, the Don made tolerably habitable, furnishing a good bed, in an old barrack of a room. It had formerly been the residence of a nobleman, but the constant thoroughfare of the French had long since caused its owner to quit the country, leaving at the mercy of the plundering crew his property and his dwelling. The wreck and havoc which were made upon his furniture, and the interior of the mansion, fully justified the fears of its original possessor.

On the 1st of September, we again resumed our journey towards the interior; and, marching some hours before daylight, we arrived when it became clear, at La Hava. Our road, for the most part, lay over a country thinly planted with olive trees, but producing numerous fruitful vines. On approaching La Hava, the distant spires of Don Benito became discernible, and, on passing two leagues further, appeared the mountain of Marcella, upon the highest part of which stands the castle and village of Marcella. The former is an old fortified ruin, having a round tower in the centre, and the latter a poor miserable place, consisting of a few wretched hovels crowded together.

Like all the small towns, in this part of Spain, we found La Hava a collection of insignificant habitations, thrown into a groupe, without order or regularity, as if the place had suddenly dropped from the clouds; the chapel, as usual, in the centre, being the most prominent object in this confused assemblage of nondescript dwellings.

We entered Don Benito on the 4th of September, and, as we had been formerly quartered there, the inhabitants were kind and hospitable. In this instance, as well as in every other, when we had occasion to make the observation, the Spaniards proved themselves a generous and friendly people, evincing in every possible way, and by every mark of good-will, the pleasure they experienced not only in seeing strangers but on the return of those whom they had known before, and who had at other times enjoyed their hospitality. I was quartered at the house of Don Pedro Montenegro, a fat portly gentleman, who, with his family, exerted themselves to make my residence within their walls as agreeable as I could desire.

During our stay the ceremony of a Spanish wedding was performed in my quarters, which, though not affording much that was calculated to enliven the company assembled, was characteristic of the people, and their motives for entering into the holy state. Alonzo, the happy bridegroom, was a rosy cheeked comely boy of sixteen. His friends proposed him as a suitable match for Senora Maria Teresa, the daughter of my landlord, for the purpose of preventing his being liable to be called off to serve in the armies—married men being then exempt from the contributions required to fill up the ranks, all the youthful fellows in the neighbourhood espoused themselves in order to avoid the Junta's levies; so that many contracted an union at a very early age, or when mere children, for fear of the war.—Our hero did not appear to be much interested about the matter; young and simple, as he was, the passion of love was quite a stranger to his breast. His intended Mariceta, a fine girl of eighteen, was however of no such temperament, for having arrived at years of discretion she was better educated in all those sort of things, and consequently made herself as engaging as possible in the eyes of her juvenile bridegroom.—They were seldom together before their marriage; courtship seemed to be laid aside as a superfluous piece of business, and the whole affair of matrimony, being previously settled by the wiseacres of their families, the poor devoted victims had nothing to do but just get on as they were commanded.

The friends and acquaintances, consisting of a bevy of old and young of both sexes, together with a moderate share of clerigos, being assembled, Alonzo made his *entrée* clothed in a *capote,* of materials warm enough to raise a flame within his frigid breast, if there was even an expiring ember there. His hair was tied up with ribbons, and a sash completed his attire. The fair bride, attended by her sister Catalina, soon came after, dressed in sable robes, that being the costume worn at all times on these occasions.

The reverend priest followed, and without delay began to make his preparations for rivetting the chain, by reading out of a huge black book, by the light of a long wax taper. Having muttered for some minutes, in a hollow tone scarcely audible, he joined their hands, then poured forth his last benediction, and so this important ceremony was concluded. After the venerable Father had bestowed his blessing on the guests around, all immediately resumed their places, on low forms and chairs on either side of the room. The Patrona, together with her assistant deities, retired to an adjoining alcoba, where they commenced serving out refreshments, of all varieties, upon large plates: these were handed about by a couple of jolly, good-looking padres, who, as they offered them to the lovely senoritas, showed no small degree of gallantry, passing off compliments and soft words, highly acceptable to their willing ears.

Poor Alonzo, meanwhile, sat like Patience, and, though not smiling at grief, yet he looked very much as if he would rather be at home with his mother, than be brought to cut such a figure in the mummery. The bride, every now and then, modestly hid her face and blushes from the vulgar gaze, under a long black veil of the finest lace.

Chocolate and cakes were handed round, and

the damsels pocketed the fragments, which they purloined without any remorse of conscience. About nine o'clock the company began to separate, and this most stupid of all stupid weddings was finished by a general salutation on all sides, and by Alonzo, amidst the smiles and winks of the envious spinsters, going off quietly to his father's, while his cara sposa remained at home in single blessedness, to dream of happiness yet to come.

While we remained at Don Benito, the natives vied with each other in their efforts to afford as much enjoyment as possible to their guests. Balls and other festivities were among the many sources by which they endeavoured to amuse us.

The assemblies were usually held in the spacious apartment of a large building, the residence of a marquis, and situated in the grand square. The fair and lively daughters of my host were regular attendants at the ball-room, and were escorted thither by a tall black looking man, who, in his official capacity of chaperon, on this and other occasions, took the damsels under his wing, and as he proceeded along collected a reinforcement of old and young; his party, by the time of their arrival, having accumulated to a motley crowd of votaries, including domestics and a train of followers: many of them under pretence of being brothers, friends or relations, intruded uninvited, pushing after the ladies without ceremony, to the no small annoyance of the respectable portion of the company. The women on those occasions make but few preparatory arrangements. After having merely plaited up the hair, or thrown a mantilla loosely across the neck and shoulders, and adorned the feet with a pair of white or yellow shoes, they sally forth in the same dress which they have worn during the day.

We departed from Don Benito on the 13th of September, and passing over the plains of Medellin, forded the Guadiana about a league above the bridge.

On the 14th we reached Villa Mercia. It was so very early when we got into the neighbourhood of this place, a place so wretched that we could scarcely get even a drop of water. The troops halted on the open ground some distance from the village. The vestige of a single plant or tree was not to be seen on any side, and the dry stubble-fields yielded us no means of obtaining the comfort of a fire. Our chances for a breakfast were therefore but slight. After marching for the greater part of a very cold night, we all looked blue enough at daybreak, eyeing wistfully the country round for something to build our hopes upon; but alas! the interminable waste was to us as much a desert as the barren sands of Africa. When the arms were piled the men threw off their packs, and seating themselves thereon, commenced a voyage of discovery in their haversacks, rummaging every hole and corner for sundry fragments, the residue of four days provender. The officers with hollow cheeks and cadaverous aspect, having gone to bed, (or rather to mach,) supperless, and being without the slightest chance of muffins or hot rolls, were ruminating on the evil day on which they went a soldiering. In the midst of this, some of the knowing hands, while prowling about the camp, for a few sticks wherewithal to boil a kettle, beheld an old, crazy and dismantled bullock-cart, (on the retired list) lying quietly on the field. As soon as the prize was seen, a general rush succeeded, and, like a pack of hounds pouncing on an unfortunate fox, they flew at the ill-fated remnant of the waggon, and without waiting to dissect, *secundem artem*, the subject before them, they tore it limb from limb, and the broken fragments were carried off in triumph by the ravenous crew.

Soon there arose a thin curling smoke in various quarters, awfully distant from each other, and those lucky favourites of fortune, who got a splinter of the aforesaid vehicle, were quickly gladdened by a flame; meanwhile, the tin, wherein the Congo was infused, hung dangling on a ramrod, suspended by two bayonets stuck cunningly in the earth. The poor wretch, with a visage of at least a span in length, who failed in his attempts to share in the spoil of the waggon, scraped up the stubble, which, damp with heavy dew, baffled all his labour, and he was at last obliged, with his culinary vessel in one hand, and his canister in the other, to wander from right to left, in order to beg a portion of some friendly blaze.

Renewing our march on the following day, we continued on the road until a late hour.—The face of the country, as far as the eye could reach, was an extended waste, devoid of any thing in the shape of tillage; the plain, wide and boundless, interspersed with scattered rocks, with occasional patches of heath and broom, was quite as wild as any lover of romance could wish. After some hours travelling over this dreary road, its sameness was at length relieved by a view of the Sierra de Santa-Cruz, the highest pinnacle of which rises in the form of a pyramid, and has a most remarkable-looking old castle, situated upon a lofty cliff near its western side.

The main road from Villa Mercia directed us, after many turnings, to the base of those heights. Among the rocks even to the highest peak, the sheep and goats were browsing, and at intervals we observed the shepherds with their dogs, in places where it would seem impossible that any human being could obtain a footing. In the grassy marshes below were large herds of oxen and other cattle grazing.—We had an opportunity of having a nearer view of these shepherds, who descended from the steep acclivities, and we were astonished beyond measure at their ferocious aspect and savage garb; one could not help comparing them, as they stood, with those of old, as described by ancient writers, when in simple dress, with crook and pipe, the rustics tending their flocks in Arcadian fields, charmed by soft and rural notes the lovely damsels of the woods and plains. The Spanish guardian of the flock, from his war-like costume, his dark and bearded visage, seemed better adapted for a ruffian robber of the forest, or the ranks of a Guerilla Chief, than a gentle warbler of simple love songs. These peasants were cloathed with coarse materials; their inner garments were protected from the weather by pieces of sheep skin rudely joined, and they were armed with a dirk and an old fusil.

On the 29th of September we departed from Guerindote, our route leading over the spacious plain that extended to the Tagus. Upon the green borders of that river we at length arrived, and before us, in the midst of splendid scenery, lay the far-famed City of Toledo. The inhabitants, on first beholding our approach, assembled in multitudes on the road, near the outskirts, where we had already halted. They pressed on to welcome us, while with loud huzzas and shouting they rent the air. We entered by the principal gate, and marched up to the Plaza Mayor, amidst joyous salutations, and the ringing of innumerable bells. The balconies around were literally crammed with a brilliant show of beauty, waving flags, handkerchiefs and ribbons; their delight on seeing the English soldiers, was expressed with unaffected gladness, and could we judge by this display of feeling, we might have flattered ourselves with at least having the people of this city for our friends.

Toledo, from its situation on a semicircular chain of rugged heights, has a broken and irregular aspect; and, as the steep sides of the eminence descend precipitously to the Tagus, many of the buildings seem as it were impending over the banks of that river, which nearly surrounds the city walls. Across the stream are two solid bridges, each having one arch of considerable span, and of dimensions correspondent to the magnitude of the passage.

The brief period of our stay permitted not of any minute inspection of various objects, well deserving the traveller's notice. We could therefore take but a hasty survey; and in passing through the city, it was impossible to avoid admiring the beauty of many buildings, the names of which we knew not, nor had time to enquire.

Having proceeded down the Calle del Caromen, a long and handsome street, we found ourselves close to the grand cathedral, the finest perhaps in the kingdom. The utmost force of language could but faintly convey any idea of the magnificence of that building; the grandeur of which far exceeded any thing we had hitherto beheld in this country, and was worthy of being honored by a far more minute inspection than we had time to bestow on it.

The roof is supported by lofty pillars and fluted columns of marble, and composition in imitation thereof. The floor is composed of the same stone, dark, and highly polished. Approaching towards the centre aisle, we encountered a ragged looking cicerone, who volunteered to conduct us to the vault within which lay in state the anatomy of St. Ursula, a lady whose memory is highly reverenced by the people of Spain. We descended by a narrow flight of stone steps, led on by the aforesaid genius, who, chuckling within himself at the idea of relieving the curious Inglezes of their loose cash, yet seeming wondrous grave, brought us in a few moments to the door of the sepulchre. The skeleton of her ladyship lay very comfortably in a glass case, and lest the venerable saint might feel rather solitary in this abode, a lamp was suspended from the vaulted roof of her bedchamber, to enliven her gloomy residence, as well as to enable the visitors to examine her crumbling bones.

Having rewarded the guide, we renewed our

search for the numerous objects within this extraordinary and sacred pile, and while we were thus engaged we met the Secretary, who introduced us to his apartments, where we were much gratified by the sight of some rich and beautiful paintings, by which the walls were ornamented. Among the exhibitions of art, which hung within the court yard, those of the capture of Toledo, by the Spaniards from the Moors, and the grand procession of Charles the 4th were by far the finest in the Cathedral. They were all executed by that inimitable artist Francisco Bayue. Having seen every thing worthy of observation within, we passed through the main entrance, and commenced the ascent of a flight of steps leading to the belfry; at the top of which having safely landed we beheld the famous bell, said to be the largest in Europe. It is suspended from a massive beam, and its weight, as marked on the side, is 1543 arobas of 32lb each. The height of the spire, as far as the belfry, is about two hundred feet, and we counted a hundred and ninety four steps, while climbing to this part of the tower.

The Senoras of Toledo are low in stature: but being possessed of as large a share of beauty as those of any other part of Spain, and full of animation, they are all that can be wished as far as personal charms are concerned. And, indeed, to do them every justice, I must say they received us with a warm and hearty kindness, that was long, yes, very long remembered. When they assemble on the *passeo*, they dress in every respect as they do for public worship, clothed in fine robes of the richest black silk or velvet, trimmed with lace, their persons decorated with various brilliant ornaments, and the hair tastefully braided up with combs of costly workmanship. A beautiful transparent veil, thrown gracefully over the figure, partially enfolds those charms it is intended to adorn.

Females of the lower class wear thick and substantial garments of black or brown cloth, of measurement so ample, that no opinion can be formed as to the dimensions of their shape. The men of rank generally dress in black, with chapeau, buckles, sword, and waistbelt. The working people and peasants wore the cloth jacket, botas, and montero cap, with a profusion of tassels and buttons. Instead of shoes they wear sandals, made of strong brown leather, laced round the foot and instep; these, together with the botas, (or leathern gaiters), shew to great advantage their round and well turned limbs.

We departed from Toledo on the 30th of September, at an early hour in the morning, very much regretting that we had so short a time to see every thing worthy of notice in that delightful place. Our route lay through a richly planted vale, watered by the Tagus, with whose rapid current we were in company for the whole of this day's march.

Towards evening the troops were encamped upon a most inviting spot; the ground upon which our alignement was taken up being the fresh and verdant banks of the river, and around our bivouac, on every side, were gardens and green plantations, filled with a great variety of shrubs and flowers in their Autumnal tints. With the soft leaves of these, (now thickly fallen), for a bed, we enjoyed that rest, after a toilsome journey, which "the weary traveller never seeks in vain."

In the forenoon of the 1st of October, the column was again on the main road leading to Aranjuez, and parallel with the course of the river. When we were within two leagues of our destined quarters, we entered a noble avenue of tall trees, their branches forming a long continued archway overhead, and protecting us from a scorching sun. The camino real was planted in double rows, in so direct a line, that the endless vista in perspective was, to our impatient optics, any thing but agreeable; and whatever little stock of patience remained within our keeping, was pretty well exhausted by the time we gained the end of our morning's tramp. At last, about 11 o'clock, we got into our cantonments; bugles, drums, and pipes rattling through the streets, enough, (at least in one sense,) to bring the very stones about our ears. Without any unnecessary delay, we were permitted to make ourselves perfectly at home, in mansions devoid of either comfort or means of entertainment; emblems they truly were of splendid misery. The ruthless hand of French campaigning had converted this once interesting place into a comparative wilderness; the habitations had not only been pillaged, but the furniture burned or destroyed, and every vestige of their former grandeur swept away, by the cruel ravages of this devastating warfare, leaving us to dispute with rats, and other vermin, for possession of their desolate abodes.

Aranjuez, which is seven leagues from Madrid, seven from Toledo, and nineteen from Segovia, has long been the residence of the Spanish Court; and, even in its fallen state, there is still sufficient to denote its past splendour. In spite of the ruin to which it has been exposed, it has the stamp of noble bearing, and, previous to the invasion, must have been one of the most beautiful towns in the Spanish dominions. The Royal Palace, on the banks of the Tagus, is worthy of being the residence of princes, and contains a number of costly and magnificent paintings.

The Queen's Palace, or the Casa de Labrador, the charming summer retreat of her Majesty, is fitted up with simplicity and elegance combined, and, being replete with every comfort and luxury suited for a Queen, it may well be termed a paradise in miniature. The walls are covered with richly embroidered tapestry, and the finest needlework, executed on silk and velvet, of exquisite workmanship.

Around the palaces and buildings for the nobility and members of the court, are numerous gardens, groves, and plantations, in the walks through which we rambled with much delight, as often as our duties might permit. The few inhabitants remaining here assembled on the promenade, to enjoy our military music, while a sprinkling of pretty blackeyed senoritas rendered the place more highly interesting.

CHAPTER XIII.

A BROTHER officer now joined with me in forming the plan of an excursion to Madrid. We had long been anxious to examine that celebrated capital, and were therefore desirous not to miss the opportunity afforded by our near vicinity to that city, which, in all human probability, might never occur again during the period of our natural lives. We asked and obtained leave accordingly, and started, on the evening of the 9th of October, like a brace of knights errant, upon our eventful journey. The weather was fine for that season of the year, and circumstances appearing favourable to our pilgrimage we considered it advisable to proceed at a late hour, rather than wait for the following day, inasmuch as, in our uncertain mode of life, we knew not what a day might bring forth. We presumed upon our own skill to find out the way, and, trusting to that, took neither guide nor other attendant in our train, but sallied forth, mounted on a couple of hardy mules, and scantily provided with any thing pertaining to inward comfort.

Pacing along the Camino de la Reyna, a long extended avenue, we arrived, as it began to get dark, at the Queen's Bridge, a solid structure on the Tagus, whence proceeding as we imagined on the direct road to Madrid, we jogged on heartily without apprehension as to the course we followed.

The night became still more obscure and cold, and threatened rain. In the meanwhile we pursued the direction diametrically opposite to that we should have done; turning away from the main road, and leaving our animals to make choice of any particular route they might in their sagacity prefer. For some time we progressed, in a state of uncertainty as to what point of the compass we were steering towards, till at length, passing through a wide gate very invitingly open before us, we were brought to a full stop, on a wild common, destitute of any track, or vestige of even a pathway. In this awkward dilemma we were completely at a nonplus, repenting sincerely of having set forth at so late an hour upon our Quixotic expedition. To go forward at all hazards was our only remedy.

The situation was by no means an enviable one, on a dark night in October, shivering on a desolate waste, with a cheerless journey staring us in the face, or a cheerless bed on the cold earth. To add to our discomfort, we had the prospect of being exposed to the inclemency of most severe weather. It might be truly said that our experience was likely to be dearly purchased.—After an hour's fruitless exertion to get out of the labyrinth in which we had involved ourselves, we at last heard the barking of some dogs, and immediately advanced towards the quarter from which the sound proceeded, and were in no small degree gratified at finding we were close to a village. We rapped most lustily at the door of the first house we came to, and hailing the landlord, implored him to take compassion on two weary travellers, and give us lodging until daylight. Our call was quickly answered by a surly voice from within, demanding our reason for disturbing his highness at that improper hour; at the same time telling, or rather bawling out, in tones denoting that we were most unwelcome visitors, the disagreeable intelligence, that we were far from the high road, and should not be able to find it during the night.—The Spaniard, however, directed us to some farm houses for more intelligence, and, glad to get from this inhospitable don, who treated us as though we had been house breakers, we again began to explore the unknown region, looking out most wistfully for something by way of a clue, to obtain the object of our search. Fortunately we perceived, after much marching and countermarching, a light twinkling through the gloom and mist around us; and, struggling along over hedge, ditch, and drain, our faithful quadrupeds carried us safely to the entrance of a poor hamlet called Villa Conejo. Here the peasants were all comfortably wrapped up in their beds. With some difficulty, however, by dint of both threats and bribes, we succeeded in procuring a guide, who buckling on his garments, and taking up a formidable staff, trudged before us with boldness equal to the renowned Sancho Panza himself. We were assured of getting into the right direction before morning, and, therefore, as the time of our absence was very limited, we hesitated not to push onward, notwithstanding the lateness of the hour, in preference to quartering in the village, where, for any thing we knew to the contrary, the people might think proper to be *quartering* us in another way, not quite so agreeable to our taste, before they suffered us to depart.

In this mountainous district, the inhabitants of remote valleys are, in many cases, either brigands themselves, or closely allied to such;

hence the necessity of being on the *qui vive*, and our fears were fully justified by the fierce and bandit looking aspect of those dark fellows who made their appearance on our arrival. With sinister looks and angry scowls, they glanced at us in a manner that made us rejoice to get away, chusing rather to encounter the howling winds than the treachery of those suspicious gentlemen. Having no particular desire to feel the sharp edge of their knives, that peeped from beneath their girdles, we wisely pursued our journey in quest of new adventures, and prepared for any rough work which might be in reserve.

Led on by our gallant pioneer, we once more faced the storm, and, groping forward amidst the darkness, we pushed our way through the intricate and trackless waste. Our trusty mules, following the footsteps of the guide, carried us safely over the ground, proving how much we owed to those poor animals for the service they afforded. About midnight we passed the moorland, and arrived at a miserable village, consisting of a few wretched hovels, scarcely offering the privilege of shelter from the violence of the blast. Into one of these we gained admittance, and, after some little parley with the landlord, we were honoured with permission to stretch our wearied limbs on a flinty bed, manufactured from rough materials, and thrown upon a floor that had long been unswept by brush or broom. Our whiskered aid-de-camp, having consigned us to the protection of the patron, gathered himself up within the ample folds of his cloak, and rolled into the chimney corner, where his nasal machinery was set agoing, and soon produced an overture sufficient to banish sleep from the most drowsy eyelids.

About 4 o'clock, we rose from our comfortless mattress, and, without any unnecessary delay in the adjustment of the toilet, resumed our journey northwards. On the first appearance of daylight, we descended from the mountain path, and arrived near the little village of Bayone, situated on the right bank of the river Guarena.

After passing through the small towns of Cienposuelo and Valdemoro, we at length gained the extremity of the avenue or approach from Aranjuez, and here, for the first time, we beheld the towers and elevated buildings of Madrid. Crossing the Manzanares by the Puente de Toledo, we entered the Calle de Toledo, a steep narrow street, which conducted us to the Grand Square, from whence going into a small central space, called Le Plaza de Porte del Sol, we brought up at the doors of a tavern, under the sign of La Fonda François. Here we enjoyed an excellent breakfast; our hostess, a garrulous dame, knew well how to charge for the demands made upon her larder, by appetites sharpened on the touch-stone of eight leagues; and, judging from our meagre aspect, that our performances as trenchermen would be of no despicable order, she determined that her pocket at least should be no loser by our morning's ride.

The Alcalde with his satellites and myrmidons gave us considerable trouble, teazing us with numerous questions, as well as a strict cross-examination with regard to our object in coming here; and I verily believe that, had we not been dressed in British uniform, they would have furnished us with lodgings in a building not quite in accordance with our ideas of freedom, or suitable to our state of mind.— They, however, in a most ungracious manner, gave us billets on the house of a wealthy Spaniard, living in the Calle del San Antonio, which is a handsome street leading from the Grand Square. In these quarters we enjoyed the comforts of a civilized life, for a short term after the wandering and vagrant system of the bivouac, or encampment; and we made good use of the interval allowed in viewing the *lions* of this extraordinary place, and in exploring every hole and corner that was likely to contain anything marvellous or worthy of observation.

Manifold accounts have been given by sundry tourists respecting Madrid; in order therefore to avoid all useless repetition, I shall merely glance at a few matters, which may, perchance, have escaped the notice of these curiosity hunters.

Our patron, Don Pedro Gonzalez, was a civil and obliging personage; but as we had good reason to know that he was in the French interest, we suspected that his conduct was not sincere, and we were the more confirmed in this opinion, from the very marked attention paid by him to a certain Madame, of vivacious manners, named Durand. The worthy Don being a bachelor, appearances favoured the rumour, that an intimacy of a more binding nature was likely to take place between them; or, in other words, the love-stricken Pedro was about to become a Benedict. To be on good terms with Mademoiselle was therefore equivalent to the same happy circumstances with regard to our host, who, accordingly, gave every facility to our exertions in gaining admittance to public places; and was, on various opportunities, highly useful to his guests. The conversation and agreeable disposition of the gay Frenchwoman served to dissipate any melancholy thoughts that might have haunted us. Without being decidedly handsome, she had a very good set of features, and was of such a pleasant temperament, that, although she was arrived at a reflecting age, her society was courted by many admiring swains, to the no small annoyance of the gallant Lothario himself, whose chief motive, in acting the part of our Cicerone, was, that he might withdraw the Officiales Ingleses from any temptation that might be presented to our susceptible hearts, by the wily blandishments and ensnaring charms of his lovely *dulcinea.*

The principal places of amusement open at this time were the Opera House, in the Calle de Principe, and the theatre denominated El Collegio de la Cruz. What a college might have to do with the name of theatre, I could not imagine, unless it were that the loose and dissipated habits of collegians in general favored those entertainments, or that the members of the learned institutions at Madrid were the chief patrons of the stage. The house was opened at an early hour, and filled by a respectable though motley audience. Among the singular customs of Spain is that of placing the ladies and gentlemen at a most awful distance from each other; a custom which in our minds would have been more honoured in the breach than in the observance; and if we might be permitted to judge from the bewitching glances of their sparkling eyes, the fair senoritas would have had no sort of objection to a repeal of such an unnatural *disunion.* Had the performances been ever so delightful, they must of necessity, have proved " flat, stale and unprofitable," to the senses of gentlemen, banished as we were by such an abominable regulation from all intercourse or communion with that portion of the assembled audience in which was comprised all that was lovely and beautiful in nature's fair creation. The lunetta (or pit,) resembled a den or arena of wild men of the woods—such were the characters inclosed therein untamed by female influence.—The noisy crew maintained such a loud and boisterous turmoil, that it was impossible to hear one word that was uttered on the stage, and the scene enacted in the pit or lunetta was something not unlike the performances in a bear garden.

The balcos (or boxes,) fronting the stage,

were occupied by the ladies, who, decked out in costly attire, manœuvred their fans with such activity, that they might have literally been said to have answered all the purpose of the eastern *punka*;* a cool and refreshing air being thus circulated throughout the crowded building. The house was but dimly illumined by some dirty lamps, scantily furnished with oil. The music was tolerably good, although somewhat marred by the rude accompaniment from our friends in the lunetta. The play went off with vociferous applause, though the performers knew scarcely a word of their parts —but, owing to the noise, pantomime answered just as well. The prompter, an ugly caitiff, with black bushy whiskers, and a woolly head encased within a greasy velvet cap, was stuck up before the footlights, with half his body above the level of the stage, as if about to emerge from the bowels of the earth, like some dæmon from the nether region, while he, with

* The punka, used in India, is an enormous kind of fan, suspended in a room, and moved by ropes, to cool the air.

angry looks and threatening gesture, endeavoured to hammer into the impenetrable skulls of the stupid actors the words intended for their delivery.

About 11 o'clock the entertainment was concluded; and we returned to our lodgings escorted by a crowd of ragged boys, carrying flambeaux to light us home. The Theatre De la Cruz, though smaller than that of Del Principe, is ornamented with better taste, and is on the whole a handsome building. In both the performers are tolerable, and the dancing in the little theatre is beautiful beyond description. The expense of admission amounts to nearly the same as in England. There were no other places of amusement open during our stay.

Assemblies and private concerts were held in various parts of the city; but since the war with France all public balls and concerts have been discontinued. The famous bull-fights, deemed the most enlightened exhibitions of modern times by the natives, were held on Mondays and Fridays in the Plaza Mayor, or Plaza de Torres.

Notwithstanding the unsettled state of things the inhabitants of Madrid seem to enjoy life to the fullest extent, and in the constant pursuit of gaiety endeavour to dispel that gloom which would otherwise pervade their city, and in which those of any other capital would be involved. They appeared to act with the same indifference and unconcern, when the French or British were in possession, and of those two nations I believe the majority of them preferred the former, which, if one may judge from the natural levity and liveliness of their disposition, proceeded not only from their love of show, but from similarity of manners, taste and habits. With the Spanish fair in particular the French were the greater favourites, having, by their gallantry and politeness, during their long residence, won golden opinions, and gained a place in their confidence and esteem.

After visiting the Royal Palace, (a description of which I dare not enter into, because the time for observation was much too short, we proceeded to an edifice called La China, a fortified place, and where the celebrated porcelain and China ware had been manufactured. A train of gunpowder having been laid, preparatory to blowing up the works, no person was admitted within, nor do I think there was any particular inducement to press for entrance.—From a general glance at its exterior, there appeared nothing to recommend it, for either beauty or grandeur of effect. It is a plain building, of white stone, situated on an eminence beyond the Retiro, commanding the principal part of the city and its environs.

The Palace of the Retiro was not worth seeing, being merely a ruinous square of low buildings, lately converted into a barrack, and having within its limits a large and spacious court yard. It was palisaded and strongly defended by works, which were considerably strengthened by the French. Close to the entrance, is the Palace of Godoy, Prince of the Peace, which faces the Prado, the great public

Alameda of Madrid. The fabric, notwithstanding its limited scale, is furnished in a most costly and splendid style, and contained a large collection of rare and beautiful paintings.

In point of magnificence it is equal, if not superior, to the Casa de Campo, a country residence for the Royal Family, near the Manzanares.

After seeing the Royal Museum, (which, like all other museums, is well filled with objects deserving the attention of the curious,) we visited the armoury, (near the gate of Saint Barbara) stiled here El Real Parque d'Artilleria, where valuable specimens of ancient armour, and many plans and models, were exhibited. Some thousand stand of arms were piled in harmless quietude, and arranged with order and regularity.

King Joseph and his retinue thought proper to make free with the carriages and other means of conveyance of the people of Madrid, with which they drove off, leaving the owners to trudge about in a more humble manner than they had hitherto been used to. The fair Senoras were thus reluctantly compelled to tramp the pavé, exposing their graceful and fascinating persons to the rude gaze of a vulgar multitude.

On arriving at the extremity of the Calle de Alcala, we found ourselves on that delightful mall called the Prado, already mentioned, which is an avenue about half a mile in length; it is planted on each side with uniform rows of various trees, whose branches are interwoven through the greater part of the year. This promenade is kept in the highest order, and between the double line of trees are gravel walks, enclosed by shrubs and evergreens. At each end is a fountain of the finest polished marble, the sculpture of which is executed in the most beautiful manner. Here the Royal Family, as well as the nobility and gentry, assemble for the passeo at the fashionable hours; to the lower classes the walk is open at all periods.

They are an active and bustling people here, the various occupations going on with a degree of spirit not easily accounted for in these troublesome times. The number of poor, however, is very great; many dying in the streets of starvation. We met several persons, male and female, who had formerly been possessed of wealth and distinction, endeavouring to obtain a livelihood by selling, in a private way, different articles of their dress and household furniture. Others, particularly women, whose looks bespoke their having lived in better days, were reduced to the miserable situation of vending pamphlets or small wares, or keeping stalls, or even hawking salt fish or vegetables through the city.

Madrid was walled in ancient times; no vestige, however, now remains of any such defences, it is completely open and exposed.

We now prepared for our departure to Aranjuez; and, therefore, for any further information about Madrid, I must direct the reader's attention to the recent works on Spain and its capital, wherein will be found, in detail, the best accounts of all that is worthy the traveller's notice. I cannot, however, avoid saying something of the mode of access to their dwellings, which, from the difficulty caused by this mode, might almost have been called forbidden ground. The houses of Madrid are solid, and furnished as usual with balconies and prison-like windows, and are sometimes of great magnitude; those of the Alcade, and the Governor Don Inacio Cortabunio, forming one side of a tolerably long street. Within the entrance of the great door is usually a small rectangular passage, from whence the ascent to the upper part of the building is gained by a narrow flight of stone steps. On arriving at the extremity of the hall or passage just mentioned, a strongly bolted door, which shuts in the staircase, forbids your further approach; but, after considerable delay, you discover a small bellcord, which you pull, and then another trial of your patience takes place, and you remain still cooling your heels, at the end of a cold dark place, not unlike a cavern. Your solitude is at length disturbed by the sepulchral tone of an old weather-beaten Sybil, who, peering with an ugly, wizened, and vinegar countenance through a wicket or small crevice overhead, screams out, with shrill and angry voice, "qui quiere!" while, at the same time, doubtful of your rank or character, she scans with the hideous glances of an evil eye the bearings of your person. When you have satisfied her on this head, she, much against the grain, raises the unwilling latch by means of a greasy rope. When the massive portal, creaking on its rusty hinges, is pushed open, not without much force, and you find yourself upon the gloomy steps to grope as best you can to the upper regions, your advances are still impeded, either by the threats of the garrulous antique, or by the barking of some furious Cerberus, a fit companion for his sister guardian of the dwelling. When you are known, and become familiar, the mode of admittance is by no means a work of so much difficulty, nor is the frosty visaged Argus so jealous of access.

CHAPTER XIV.

We arrived at Aranjuez on the 13th of October, after an absence of four days; three of which were spent as agreeably as we could have wished, and in the full enjoyment of every variety afforded by a city well deserving a longer visit, and one which though it is less generally known, is more interesting in every point of view, than many that are more frequently resorted to.

On the 23rd of October the troops were again in full march, on the high road to Madrid, halting at various intermediate stations. We passed that city, on the 29th of the same month, and, tantalized as we were by our close proximity to its gates, we continued onward in the direction of the Pass of Guadarama, it being the object of our chief to follow hard upon the French army, (which was then bending northward, in rapid strides,) and allow them no rest, night or day, until we brought them to a decisive combat. Our road, as we approached the mountains, lay over a fertile country; the view on every side presenting a vast extent of arable and tillage land. Towards evening, after a long and painful journey, we halted at the Court-yard of the Escurial.

This famous palace, built by Philip the Second of Spain, is consecrated to St. Lawrence, and is formed after the pattern of a gridiron, upon which very useful culinary article the Saint is supposed to have undergone the operation of being broiled. The building stands on one of the heights at the base of the lofty chain of the Guadarama, and is a huge and spacious pile, enclosing four distinct court yards, the whole surrounded by an extensive range of buildings, allotted to the domestic establishment of the royal household. The grand entrance faces the mountain, the barren sides of which offer but a confined and uninteresting prospect. From the windows of the principal apartments, looking to the South, (which are said to be as numerous as the days in the year,) a view embracing all that fine extent of country round Madrid, and along the Manzanares, may, however, be enjoyed, which fully compensates for the dull uniformity on the other quarters. Some idea may be formed of the enormous amplitude of the structure, when it is considered that General Hill's division, including the Portuguese troops, were lodged within the walls, and found sufficient room in the galleries, court-yards, and outer-halls, without entering any of the private chambers. Our brigade marched up the great staircase, with ample space to move along in sections. It was a splendid cantonment, and worthy a better fate than that of being converted into a barrack and cooking place for a few thousand hungry soldiers.

The rooms, into which the officers obtained admittance, were spacious and lofty, those appropriated to the members of the court being ornamented and furnished in a costly manner. The lateness of our arrival, as well as the shortness of our stay, prevented our seeing the mausoleum; in which the royal family of Spain has been entombed for ages past. It is considered one of the greatest curiosities in Europe, and is beneath the grand chapel of the palace. The grand front has three separate entrances, and above the dome surmounting the central gate, the figure of St. Lawrence, together with the gridiron, stand upon a pedestal, and underneath are the Arms of Spain.

On the 1st of November we moved on towards the crest of the Guadarama, our route being along the summit of the hills, forming the lower branches of the Sierra, the ascent of which we took more than two hours to accomplish; many times on the way being obliged to halt, in order to gain breath for a further stretch. It was a work of considerable fatigue to both men and animals, and on arriving at the extreme point we were fairly exhausted by the effect of our morning's walk. Nature has here placed a formidable barrier between the provinces of Old and New Castile. This road, which is the only one across the mountain, is difficult of access, the rocks on either side being steep, rugged, and in some parts perpendicular, rising high above the causeway. Close to where we halted stands a pedestal of granite, on which is placed the figure of a lion crouched, holding between his paws two balls, intended, as denoted by the inscription underneath, to represent the provinces below. In the centre of the pedestal is inserted a square slab of marble, on which is inscribed, in large characters, "Fernando VII, Pater Patriæ," followed by a long account of the cause for which the monument was erected, but in letters so small, and so much defaced, that it is a matter of some difficulty to decipher the mysterious tale.

Being again formed into something like marching order, we proceeded downward with a lively pace, leaving the plains of New Castile behind, and bidding a long and last farewell to that part of Spain, which had been for years gone by the theatre of our varied and ofttimes not very peaceful occupation. On our descent from the Sierra, we continued along the main road to Valladolid, and after having cantoned at several intermediate stages, arrived on the 8th at Alba de Tormes, a small town, one day's march from Salamanca, and commanding the passage of the Tormes, over which, at this place, there was a solid stone bridge.

We were soon actively employed getting all the old walls and defences into good condition, and, after waiting behind them for a few days, expecting an attack from a large body of the French army, (who had sent some round shot about our ears), we again crossed the river, taking care to destroy the bridges, the moment that the last of our men were over.

The enemy, who had threatened in so formidable a way, sheered off to his left, making for the road to Ciudad Rodrigo, in order to interrupt our progress in that line, with the view of eventually cutting off our communication with the frontiers of Portugal.

The whole of the British forces, meanwhile, passed on towards the Aripiles, those remarkable heights, where the great contest of Salamanca was fought in the preceding year. Here battle was again offered to the French, who declined the pleasure of our kind invitation, and wisely deeming prudence to be the better part of valour, continued their manœuvres to impede our march on Portugal, and succeeded in getting possession of almost all the approaches in that direction.

On the 14th, our troops were rapidly pushed forward, in order to counteract their plans, and, by forced marches, we got the lead, the foremost columns being far advanced on the road to Rodrigo in the course of that day. It was a neck and neck concern, and nothing but the superior generalship of Lord Wellington could have brought us through the difficulty.

The rain poured down in torrents, as we entered the woods, through which the various routes penetrated, and the most inclement weather that ever was experienced set in on the commencement of this unfortunate march.

Wind and hail in all their varieties beat unmercifully upon us, and the elements in fearful agitation combined to assail us on every side, while the roads, broken up by the violence of the storm, were rendered almost impassable, producing thereby the utmost delay in the transport of our supplies. To increase our sufferings, the personal baggage had been sent on some days in advance, so that we had no covering whatever but the garments that we wore, which were now waxing quite deplorable; and as for subsistence, our only resource was the miserable contents of a lank and scanty haversack, wherein were jumbled up together, in a sort of medley, the various remnants of ration leather, (falsely called beef), and mouldy biscuit, hard and jaw breaking, of which the maggots contended for a share.—It was enough to horrify the poor chop-fallen wanderer, who trudged along most dismally, cold, drenched, and woebegone.

Were I to relate but one tenth of the sufferings we endured, in what is known as the retreat of Salamanca, civilians would stare, and say that I dealt largely in the marvellous, or was drawing a long bow; but, start not, ye fireside and ye featherbed gentry, when I inform you, that many times have we arisen from our damp, and comfortless berth on the cold ground, with no prospect of a breakfast, but that which we derived from a meal of acorns, and often have we munched at these in lieu of more savoury food; chewing (by way of dessert), the bitter cud of disappointment and vexation.

At the termination of each day's march, down came the branches of the forest, and loudly clashed the bill hook and the axe, to put in requisition materials for the long wished-for fire, to establish which was a labour of no trifling nature, for the timber, throughly saturated with rain, lay in smoking heaps, long after the light had been communicated, while we with haggard looks stood collected round the smouldering pile. The flames at length got up, all due advantage was taken of this blessing, and no sirloin was ever more industriously turned by the hand of anxious cook than were our precious bodies, both front and rear alternately, with the vain hope of getting dry, and some degree of heat wherewith to cheer our wearied bones.

In the midst of all our extremities there was still something to excite the mind; while camping out among the oak trees, numerous droves of wild pigs ran to and fro, as we invaded their dominions, and in their flight many were fired at and shot by the famished soldiers, who were ignorant, when committing the depredation, of its being a crime which would cause the displeasure of our Chief.—Some were performing the achievement of hunting down the grunters, while others displayed their skill in the culinary art, after the chase was over. The unfortunate swinish multitude afforded some delicate tit bits, and the greasy provender was bolted in solid pieces by the half-starved men.

Before we came to break in on their retirement, the poor animals were revelling in luxury on the acorns, by which they chiefly fed, but as our troops approached their haunts they set up a grand concert, resounding through the woods, the most audible tone of which was a firm thorough bass.

The hog is by no means the most despicable of the brute creation, for have we not had the learned pig, and the pig-faced lady, who thought it no disgrace to bear a likeness to the useful beast. We have moreover good reason to know that the quadruped has proved a subject of deep meditation to more than one biped. There was a certain wiseacre, who lived not quite a hundred miles from Chester, of ample paunch, and who not only loved his port, but his port loved him; for it shone in rosy blossoms on his well bronzed visage; in fact, his person bore no bad resemblance to a well filled bottle. He was a great admirer and disciple of Kitchener, Mrs. Glass, and others of the same stamp. Having one day a party at his house, he, by way of entertaining them, led them through his grounds, and, after that, to the various buildings for his cattle. "But now," says the happy man, as they approached the piggery, rubbing, at the same time, his hands with joy, "you will see something on which you may feast your eyes;" and, on giving the signal, a regiment of fat hogs were marched out of their quarters, and passed in review before the delighted guests. One of the gentlemen remarked what amazingly fine animals they were. "Yes," says their host, "I thought you would say so! I flatter myself," (here his eyes sparkled in triumph,) "there are not such prime ones in England; they ought to be so,—I feed them well,—*I have made them my constant study all my life.*"

What an intellectual scholar! there was the feast of reason with a vengeance; fat pork, tusks, bristles and all. What a study!—O ye classics, ye national educationists, ye Broughamites,—hide your diminished heads! Here's a college course for ye; aye, and one that may be studied by John Bull with joy and pride; for, instead of wasting the midnight oil, he may consult his lard-er, and contemplate, with a rapturous sensation, the Essays of Bacon, and Hog's-tales, while poring over the whole range of his swinish library. But, enough! we must recommence our march.

The gentlemen with the blue coats not chusing to measure swords with us, we lingered not upon the road, but, moving on the Agueda, arrived at the village of Robledo on the 18th. Here we were comparatively in luxury for a season: the severity of our recent journey, added to the miseries of night exposure under such dreadful weather, rendered doubly welcome the comfort of a roof; and the kitchen fire of even an humble dwelling restored us once more from our torpid state to spirit and animation. To each of the officers was allotted a tolerably good sized cabin, furnished plentifully with straw, in which, to our dismay, we found a numerous tribe of nimble footed gentry, which have already been more than once mentioned.

We broke up from those cantonments, and, steering our course over a long mountainous ridge, we entered the town of Coria, on the 30th of November. This place is situated on a steep hill, at the base of which flows the small river Alagon, and is at no great distance from the Portuguese frontier. The country around is well planted with the olive and the vine, of the latter in particular there was then a great abundance, of the finest description, from which the most delicious wine is made.

In company with another officer, I was billetted on the house of an ancient widow, who was the most perfect shrew I ever beheld. It must have been a happy day for her unfortunate spouse, that witnessed his departure from the stormy vicinity of his termagant rib, to the more peaceful mansions of the defunct.

The heaviness of the weather, subsequent to our arrival, caused us to pass rather a dreary time, made still more sad by the death-like tolling of the cathedral bells, eternally sounding in our ears. The place is well stocked with a great variety of priests, monks, friars, and other ecclesiastics, forming a worshipful host, with ill-favoured countenances. Although their looks are meagre, their corpulent rotundity of shape proves that to mortify the body forms no part whatever of their doctrine, and that an abundance of fat things, together with a liberal supply of the vinous fluid, are by no means inconsistent with their holy calling. It is also said of them, that the worldly discussion of those affairs is much more frequently the subject of their meditation, than the comparatively irksome duty of either *prayer* or *fasting*. The best and most luscious wine, not only here, but in all parts of Spain, is denominated, in justice to the better taste of those divines, "*Priests' wine*," and is more highly valued than any other.

The Alcalde, the corporation, and the myrmidons pertaining thereto, were a mean-looking, illdressed set of fellows. The former is chosen annually from the middle classes; in some instances his worship has figured in the trade of pig-driver, butcher, or other employment of that nature.

We saw but few inhabitants of distinction here; the families of the poorer order were numerous, generally ill-looking, and badly clothed. The females, in particular, we remarked, as not being "cast in nature's finest mould;" in fact, to tell the honest truth, I must say, that we never beheld a more ugly and forbidding race of damsels. On this account, they were certainly right to hide themselves. Indeed, we seldom had an opportunity of gazing at their lovely persons; as, unless at those times when they tottered, (as they always seemed to do) to chapel, they remained chiefly within doors, enjoying the genial warmth of the brasseiro, in preference to exposing their delicate frames to the effect of the chilling blast. The usual mildness of the climate, as well as the summer heat, congenial to the Spanish fair, renders them more sensible of cold, and less capable of enduring the rudeness of December winds and frost. The transition from the close atmosphere of their dwellings to the bleak and humid air within their churches is often the means of imparting to the Senoras a pale and ghastly look, their dark and sallow aspect assuming a death-like tinge, which, combined with their usually spectral form, would indicate to the observer, that the wire drawn figures on the marble flags of the chapel were speedily to occupy a tenement of small dimensions beneath the stones upon which they knelt.

A short time subsequent to our arrival at

Coria, Colonel Charles Stewart, of the 50th, died of fever, brought on by excessive fatigue, after an illness, of about ten days. His constitution was undermined, not only by the effect of past service in India, but by that in which he was engaged in Spain. The harassing marches we had undergone since we passed the Tormes overcame his already impaired health, and he may be literally said to have fallen a victim to his unwearied exertions on that retreat.

By all who could appreciate the value of high military feeling and strict discipline, Colonel Stewart was justly regretted. Zealous and well informed on every point of duty, he knew how to estimate those qualities in others, while he held a tight rein over the careless and inattentive. Such characters as composed the Belem* Rangers he never could approve of, and

* This troop of heroes was composed of men and officers with facings of all the colours in the rainbow, and with every variety of garb. Among them were those who could not fight, as well as those who would not; and I am sorry to say, that of the latter there was a large proportion. Some, ashamed of

at all times he set his face against a certain set of men, who were very fine fellows when strutting upon parade at home, but were so careful

---

being enrolled upon its list, remained but a short time with the corps; others, vegetating in all the delights of peace and quietness, with zealous attachment to the Rangers, put off the evil hour as long as possible. Being fond of dainties, they kept within the smell of Lisbon, with its oil and garlick, the perfume of which they snuffed up with ecstacy. As for being exposed to fire, they coveted no more than sufficed for their cigars; the smoke from thence was smoke enough for them. Figuring away with the Portuguese Senoras, they were formidable cavaliers, and as their gallantry was all expended on those fair objects, they had none to spare for warlike purposes. They were fond of duty about the castle of Belem, nor had they any particular fancy to go to a distance from the Tagus. The bivouac was their horror; they eschewed the miseries of a camp; and, with regard to marching, from the caffés to the operas and back again, was, in their ideas, just as much fatigue as any gentleman ought to suffer; therefore, to call them Rangers was a sad misnomer. In order to neutralize the evil, and prevent the corps from getting rather strong, officers were placed at Abrantes, Castel Branco, and other intermediate stations, who performed the duty of whippers in. Those in general were tight hands, and if there was an officer of rank, who bore the character of being a bitter pill, he was sure to get the post, so that the poor crest-fallen aspirants for promotion in the Belemites had no chance, but were checked in their career; and unless they could duly prove that they were curtailed in natural dimensions, by the loss of legs or arms, or had suffered other more desperate mutilations, they were forced to troop it back again, with their faces to the army.

of their own dear persons, that they kept at a most respectful distance from the field when there was any rough work going forward.

The remains of Colonel Stewart were followed to the tomb by all the troops in the garrison, and were interred in the terrace of the grand Cathedral here.

Brigadier General Wilson, late Colonel of the 39th also died here, he was an old officer and deservedly regretted.

It latterly became so difficult a matter to pass these barriers, that several preferred, though riddled through with balls, to rough it in the camp, rather than run the gauntlet past these commandants.

The worthy members of the corps above alluded to had no extraordinary relish for intelligence from the front, and when accounts came down of desperate fighting, or a hint was thrown out, that some of them might be wanted, it created a wondrous stir among them; their military ardour was cooled in a marvellous way, and whatever stock of courage they could boast of, oozed out, (as it did with Bob Acres), through their fingers' ends.

At home what capital officers they made, swarming in to join with prompt alacrity (when the war was over,) and with much bravado talking of their past campaigns, and lording it over the juniors! How they did puff and blow, in country quarters, on trooping off the guard, and looking wondrous big, as they exercised their little brief authority!

CHAPTER XV.

It was on a fine clear morning, on the 7th of January, 1813, that we departed from Coria. After marching for some hours, we passed the boundaries of a thick olive forest, about a mile beyond which appeared the large village of Monte Hermosa, so closely surrounded with trees, that the chapel spire and tiled roofs of the houses were the only discernable objects. Owing to the wildness and retirement of the situation, most of the hamlets in the forest and among the hills, are the haunts of numerous banditti, who infest the district for many leagues round. These bands of lawless men are composed chiefly of deserters from the Spanish army, joined by outcast peasants, who forming into parties resort to those heights on any sudden alarm, where concealed in caves among the rocks they lie secure from all pursuit. Armed with carbines, knives and pistols, they sally forth from their lurking-places by night, and not only plunder but frequently assassinate the unwary travellers in a most barbarous and cruel manner.

On the 17th of January I set out on a journey to Placentia, four leagues from Monte Hermosa. Being advised to travel in company with the country people, (who generally formed a numerous party,) on account of the suspicious characters above alluded to, I joined the cavalcade, and we all proceeded together. We crossed the Alagon by means of a ponderous flat-bottomed machine, answering the purpose of a ferry-boat, in which was also conveyed the mules, asses and baggage; being safely landed on the opposite bank we trotted forward at a brisk and lively pace, through the open and varied country. Having among our party a number of good-humoured buxom wenches we got on very pleasantly, for these sprightly damsels kept up such a round of merriment and noisy clatter, with occasional singing, that dullness and care with their attendant train of imps were forced to trudge it by another route, since they could get no quarter with us. The rustics, accustomed to exercise and hard labour, kept up with us, while they tramped heartily along on foot, and the women in particular, being clean-limbed, light heeled, well made and healthy, carried on with all sail ahead, to the no small surprise and admiration of their companions and fellow-travellers. After passing through a poor and hungry-looking village, we entered the wide and dark forest of Carcaboso, where the road, hitherto level, became broken and mountainous. As we approached Placentia the prospect had no redeeming feature; all was desolate and bare, and, with the exception of a few peasants here and there, as wild as the rocks upon which they stood, nothing in the shape of a living creature was visible. We descended a rough and winding path-way, (for it claimed no better name,) towards an ancient bridge by which we crossed the Jerte, and were quickly in the streets of the old town of Placentia.*

On the receipt of my billet at the Casa Consistorial, I walked thither, and found a cordial reception at the house of Francisco Barona, where, being regaled in a most excellent way, I had cause to rejoice at being quartered upon so generous a host.

---

* It was in this town that a melancholy circumstance took place on the parade of the 3rd regiment, or Old Buffs.

Lieutenant Annesley, of the grenadiers, was inspecting his company, when one of the soldiers, watching his opportunity, took his musket, and levelling it at the officer, shot him through the heart.

Annesley was a long time in the Buffs, in which he was much esteemed, and he was a remarkably good-looking young man, from the south of Ireland.

The soldier who had a pique against the Lieutenant, for some alleged ill-treatment, was a very different character, and one of those discontented sort of fellows common in every regiment; one who is usually termed by his companions a lawyer. He was shot soon after at Placentia, pursuant to the sentence of a General Court Martial.

The worthy Don was in the vale of years, and above seventy; but though infirm he had all the sprightliness of youth, and was a most agreeable and intelligent old gentleman.

His third wife, who soon made her appearance, was not more than twenty, a smart and gaily dressed senora; and the expression of her penetrating eyes afforded sufficient evidence that, as far as she was concerned, full consent might be obtained to dissolve the partnership between January and May, in order that a union more congenial to her wishes might speedily be formed. A young Spanish officer called frequently during my abode here, and from the state of affairs he appeared to be the fortunate Lothario, who was destined to perform a conspicuous part in the new treaty of alliance. Most sweetly did this son of Mars smile on the charming Leonora, who on her part, while the unsuspicious Don was fast asleep, and amusing the lovers with a nasal chaunt, discharged not a few amorous glances, intended to intangle still further the tender heart of her admiring swain.

On the 19th I pursued my journey homeward, accompanied, as before, by a numerous host of natives, returning to their several places of abode. As the night came on we again entered the forest, the travellers both horse and foot getting into close column, in order that they might be prepared to encounter any straggling party of banditti, by which these woods are sometimes infested.

While day-light continued, jovial fun and peals of laughter resounded on every side; but on the approach of darkness, the merriment and cheerful song gradually died away, and the hitherto joyous spirits were damped by the knowledge of having such troublesome neighbours in the vicinity. The old hands told many a frightful tale of murders and robberies which had been committed, serving to make the anxious listener alive to fears which were considerably increased by the frequent appearance of certain wooden crosses, erected on the spot where some unfortunate victim had been slain. The young and inexperienced, as well as those among the crowd who had not met with any dangerous adventure, looked eagerly around amidst the gloom with watchful eyes. Full of excitement and apprehension, they conjured up an ambuscade at every clump of trees; a desperado, or assassin, armed to the teeth, seemed to arise before the affrighted vision at every turning of the road; until, at length, by the time we were nearly clear through the lone and thickly-planted district, they were nearly at their wits' end, and were quite convinced that they had narrowly escaped a pilgrimage to the other world.

We fortunately gained the Alagon just as the ferry-boat was preparing to leave the bank, and, about ten o'clock, got safe into the village, after all our hair-breadth chances, without having had an interview with the outlawed wanderers, who had acted wisely in keeping at an awful distance, and not hazarding an attack upon our well-armed and formidable party.

The peasantry of Monte Hermosa are a quiet industrious race, the men are robust, black-looking fellows; their clothing is of brown cloth, over which is thrown a sort of leather covering, with an aperture for the head, worn to save the garments while occupied in the employment of wood-cutting. The women, in consequence of the ample folds of their numerous cloth coats, are wondrously capacious in the middle and lower regions, and display as prominent a rotundity as the Hottentot Venus. Had *circular sterns* been then fashionable in our navy, Sir Robert Seppings might have selected excellent models from among the females of Monte Hermosa.

The inhabitants, old and young, usually assembled after sunset in front of their houses, for the purpose of amusing themselves in a variety of ways. Their music is that of the bandeiro, a clumsy instrument, somewhat resembling a tamborine, though of a square form; it is generally played on by some ill-favoured sybil, who, beating the parchment with her skinny palm, produces a dull monotonous sound. When this is accompanied by a brace of similar hideous gorgons, catterwauling in doleful strains, the concert thus produced is not of such a very tender nature as "to soften rocks or bend the knotted oak," but a heavy hum-drum piece of discord, not unlike a funeral howl, each stanza being finished with a tedious drone by way of chorus, which has a strong relationship to the Scotch bag-pipes, and serves the purpose of a narcotic upon the admiring spectators. To this delightful harmony do the rustics trip, not on "the light fantastic toe," but with a pavior's tread, slowly moving their limbs; the stupid, sleepy and inanimate clodpoles waving at the same time their hands from side-to side, in a pendulous manner, and seeming ready to fall into the arms of their equally lifeless partner.

CHAPTER XVI.

Without the slightest degree of reluctance we departed from Monte Hermosa, on a beautiful morning, (the 8th inst.) Our road extended over that wild desert track which stretches towards the Sierra de Placentia, and proved throughout extremely bad and rugged. About twelve o'clock, after a march of two leagues and a half we got into Santivanez, and passing through that village, (which is a poor and miserable place,) we proceeded to Aggal, half a league further. Here we halted for the remainder of the day. The following morning we resumed our journey, and travelled through some romantic scenery. About a mile from the village of Gihon, we came to a remarkable old bridge, having but one arch, of immense span, its abutments being supported by the solid rocks, between whose steep and rugged sides flowed one of the tributary streams of the Alagon. The situation of this extraordinary bridge, combined with the wildness of the neighbouring country, produced on our minds an effect as impressive as it was delightful. While crossing this dangerous pass, and looking down upon the torrent that rushed furiously beneath, a terrific chasm presented itself, of at least a hundred feet in depth; and, in consequence of the slight elevation of the battlements, it required some degree of caution to avoid an awful somerset into the dark abyss.

The road, after we had safely cleared the stream, continued along the face of a craggy precipice, and at length brought us to a thick forest of oak and elm trees.

We halted at a pretty village called La Sacita

where we had good quarters; mine were at the dwelling of a respectable tiller of the ground, named Bernardo Lopez, who not only gave me a hearty welcome to his abode, but regaled me with the best of every thing that his means could afford. His better half, our worthy patrona, had spent the day at a distant town, and as in her way home she had to pass through a lawless track, the anxiety of her family for her safe return was extreme; Maricita, in particular, (the youngest daughter,) was quite unhappy on the subject, and the tears ran quickly down her very pretty and intelligent face.—The mother however soon came to the door, to the no small delight of the expectant party, and joy once more resumed its accustomed place at the social hearth of this contented family. The fire was replenished with an additional supply of fagots, and a plentiful store of plain though wholesome food was laid upon the table; in the mean time, a tribe of labouring hinds and foresters joined the group, and taking up a position in the chimney corner, made a furious attack, like hungry wolves, upon the sausages with which their platters were abundantly supplied. On the conclusion of their repast, the fair damsels of Bernardo beguiled the lazy hours with sundry cheerful ditties; but from the liberal use of garlick, onions, and other delicious things by which their breath was perfumed, the *air* of those songs, at least in one sense, was anything but ambrosial, however affecting might be the words.

We proceeded on our journey towards the mountains on the following day, and entered some very romantic scenery, unequalled in beauty, as well as grandeur of effect, by any through which we had hitherto travelled. When within a league of the Puerto de Banos, the promontory closes into a narrow pass, where a strong and almost impenetrable defile presents itself, and where a handful of resolute men could maintain the post against superior numbers. We entered the village of Banos, where we lodged that night, and marched on the succeeding day to Bejar.

After winding round the heights beyond Puerto de Banos, and about one league further, we perceived the town of Bejar, which, from its elevated site on a craggy range of hills, forms a most conspicuous feature in the surrounding scenery. The road became narrow as we approached the town, conducting in a circuitous direction along the sides of the rocky precipice, having gained the ascent of which we arrived at the gates by 2 o'clock, and proceeded through a long street to the Plaza. The balconies on each side were lined with a pretty fair display of Spanish beauty, from whose sparkling black eyes we were assailed in every quarter. They all appeared ready to leap down from the keeping of their duennas, and were so overjoyed at the sight of the first English soldiers that ever entered within their walls, that they continued one ceaseless cry of "vive los Ingleses, viva, viva," at the same time waving handkerchiefs, flags, and streamers, as we passed along.

It was easy to account for the joyful reception which we got from the inhabitants. The French were in their immediate neighbourhood, the inhabitants of the town momentarily dreaded a visit, and therefore hailed us as sent to protect them from the plundering hands of the invaders.

Bejar is situated on the crest of a barren and rocky chain of heights, branching from the mountains of Candelario. It is as large as Placentia, but differently planned, being composed of one extensive range of houses, enclosed by walls, now falling into ruin, yet still denoting that the place must have been of some importance, to have required the aid of defences such as these were, in former times.

The approach is by means of a road or pathway, difficult and bad, in consequence of the broken and irregular nature of the ground, and there are five entrances by arched gateways, leading from Salamanca, Alba, and other places. The houses are generally solid and well-built, forming a contrast with the streets, which are narrow, mean-looking, and most indifferently paved.

The 50th, which since the death of Colonel Stewart, was commanded by Lieutenant Colonel I. B. Harrison, formed the garrison here, and the 71st Light Infantry, under Colonel Cadogan, and the 92nd under Colonel Cameron, were stationed at Banos, and the neighbourhood.

In the usual routine of friendly intercourse with the natives, we experienced a good deal of what might be termed a gay sort of life; the intervals, however, and they were tolerably long, were filled up with duty enough to satisfy the most fastidious martinet, the Adjutant or Sergeant Major, with their satellites, being perpetually at our skirts, at all hours, with some newly concocted order for our edification. The French troops, under Foy, being close at hand, watching a favorable opportunity to pounce upon us when off our guard, it was quite requisite that we should be on the alert, and keep our eyes about us; idle time was, therefore, a very rare commodity, so that between pickets, outlying and inlying, parades, and other matters of an equally pleasing description, there was not any very great room left to enjoy that society which, in a most inviting way, offered its varied charms for our gratification. By reason of the miserable state of the old defences of the town, that were tumbling about our ears, it became highly necessary to guard other openings than those which the gates presented, and, accordingly, our working parties were busy night and day, in repairing, with loose stones and clay, the several chasms and breaches made by time, that yawned in the ancient and crumbling walls.

Here, and at all the other weaker points, were well armed parties stationed, and it was by no means so agreeable a lounge as that of Bondstreet, or Pall Mall, to be pacing up and down, like a hungry tiger in his cage, behind those tottering stockades, ever and anon peering above the top, to look out for squalls, or watch the motions of our vigilant opponents. It was truly no joke, or rather it was a cool one, to remain thus shivering in every limb, from the damp and frosty air of a wintry morning. The whole regiment, with the exception of the lame and lazy, was planted at their alarm post, one hour before daylight, and at the rendezvous did they remain, in awful stillness, hardly wide awake, patiently to abide the moment of dismissal, which usually came when the first glimmering of dawn was seen in the horizon, or when a white horse was visible within a mile. With faces exposed to the gentle influence of a sharp norwester, and suffering a purgatorial trial, while straining our organs of vision to get a peep at the aforesaid quadruped, we might have waited till this hour, or even to the day of doom, for no such animal appeared. However, on the full assurance that our quondam neighbours had no desire to favour us with their company at that particular period, we were again despatched from the well known rendezvous, and, hastening to our quarters, we once more unharnessed, and lost no time in bundling into the warm nest from which we had so lately started.

Among the varieties of our cantonment, assemblies were got up by those of the officers who never failed to levy war against melancholy or the spleen. Dancing was therefore the grand attraction, and the votaries of that science were amply gratified. To the lively music of our band, the charming Senoritas figured away, in all the seducing attitudes of the bolero and the waltz.

In conformity with their absurd and to us hateful usage, the fair damsels on their appearance filed off right and left, in due order, and ranged themselves along the benches with a military precision, worthy of a better cause, taking their seats at such a distance that they seemed resolved, not even in the ball-room, "to trust their soft minutes with betraying man." It was soon manifest, however, that they had not abjured the other sex, for a volley of amorous glances was darted at the forlorn and deserted males, who, taking consolation in noisy converse with each other, were soon lost amid the smoke of their offensive cigars.

With voices naturally sharp and loud, the Spanish Dons continued a palaver, that seemed as though it came through a speaking trumpet, and a Babylonish jargon arose on all sides, equalled only in the noisy purlieus of a bull-ring, while, in the mean time, when they chanced to notice any thing particularly striking or amusing in the dance, their delight and admiration were proclaimed by deafening shouts and vociferous yells. Then, again, they might be heard crying out for various changes in the figure, such as bolero! bolero! fandango! seguidillo! contradanza! each bellowing for that which pleased his own fancy, to the utter discomfiture of those who would have preferred the quiet pleasures of a less stormy region.

Fortunately, however, for us, the brawlers were seized with a gambling mania, and a rush was immediately made by them to the folding doors of an adjoining chamber, where a table was ready, covered with dollars and doubloons.

The sight of these glittering lures caused the heroes to rejoice, and attracted thereby, they crowded to the room where the blind goddess presided, leaving the party in the other to the full enjoyment of their harmless mirth, for the remainder of the night.

The ladies were highly gratified at the departure of the noisy crew, for, being vain of their graceful shapes and figures in the dance, they were happy to show them off to advantage, and to exhibit in the waltz, which, owing to the crowd, they were before unable to accomplish. Previous to the vanishing of the gamesters, great was the jostling, pushing about, and trampling of toes, amidst the hooting and noise of the spectators.

The palace of the Duke of Ossuna, near the Square, has been in its day a noble and spacious mansion. Situated on the most elevated part of the ridge, its conspicuous appearance and lofty towers impart an air of respectability to the town, that could not be derived from any other object. The solid masonry of the outer walls, together with the massive staircase and iron balustrade, which time alone can destroy, remain in good preservation; but the interior, as well as the ornamental work, are utterly in ruins, and the mutilated shell is now the only monument of its original splendour.

Round each of the windows, and the parapet of the tower, the stonework is curiously wrought in the form of a chain; and the bastion encircling each tower, together with the courtyard battlements, formed a defence in ancient times that must have added considerably to the strength and importance of the building.

There is scarcely a day in the whole year which is not dedicated to some favourite Saint, and, when the day arrives, each inhabitant, whose name is that of his Saint, considers it necessary to celebrate the great event by feasting all his friends and neighbours. St. Joseph was the protecting holy man of my landlord in Bejar, on which occasion he gave a grand entertainment to all his acquaintance far and near. The ceremony began in the morning when the family arose, and continued throughout the day. The visitors, who came to offer their gratulations and respects to my worthy host and hostess, were received in the large reception chamber occupied by Don Pepe (Joseph), and were served with cakes, chocolate, and liqueurs, handed on plated or silver salvers. Numbers came to pay their devoirs until the hour of dinner, twelve o'clock, when a glorious scene of gormandizing set in, which continued for some hours. The banquet was of a most sumptuous nature, and consisted chiefly (being

Lent time), of fish, eggs, vegetables, and many other articles in that line, cooked up into an endless variety of forms and dishes, such as omelettes, olla-podridas, pucheros, and others, which it would be tedious to enumerate. Fruit and wines were likewise dispensed in abundance, the former entering first; so that the dessert was served before the first course. To all these edibles the company did every justice, laying in with such good effect, that it would seem as if they were storing themselves with provender for a long campaign. After the siesta, which commenced at three o'clock, the remainder of the time was spent in loud conversation, in smoking, and drinking cold water. The supper, where a vigorously renewed attack was made by those hungry souls, was the last act of this gluttonous display, after which those who could accomplish it rolled away to their respective dwellings.

During the week preceding Lent, a sort of Carnival goes on throughout the town, for the entertainment of the people, who having a long fast before them give a loose rein to their carnal appetites, and such an exhibition of buffoonery takes place, that a stranger would imagine that every fool in Fernando's wide dominions had congregated here on the occasion. It is properly called El tiempo del *Trucco*, (or time for play,) men, women, and children joining in the ridiculous farce, running to and fro through the streets like maniacs, with their faces blackened, or with masks, cutting all manner of capers, and playing every variety of antics and practical jokes upon each other. The chief amusement of the mob consists in fastening on rags, bits of paper, onion skins, and other ornaments, to decorate the sternmost parts of the luckless wight to whom the honourable badges are appended. In order to complete the resemblance to the monkey race, a tail is sometimes added, giving them thereby a title to claim affinity also with their brothers of the long eared tribe. The delighted multitude, calling out "rabo, rabo," throw pails of water from the windows on the addle pate of the unfortunate pedestrian in the street, and at the same time, logs of wood tied to ropes are suddenly let fall from the balconies, to startle the passing horse or mule, so that the equestrian is soon laid sprawling on the pavement. The gazing crowd is thrown into raptures, while they grin and shout at the wry faces made by the luckless object of their mirth. This display of tom-foolery was carried on to the last moment allowed by their reverend pastors.

Besides the Rabo, they had another trick of casting about on every side a sort of weed called *pillujo*, which stuck to the clothes like flour, powdering the garments in such a manner that the streets appeared as if a fall of snow had lately taken place. In this festival the Alcalde himself, as well as other Jacks in office, took an active part. His worship, at the head of a regiment of mountebanks, rigged out in a motley sort of costume, went skipping and dancing along, while he led the noisy crew of tag-rag-and-bobtail to collect money for the support of these absurd performances.

My landlord, Don Pepe, was a worthy sort of a fellow, and gave me a good deal of information regarding the town; his brother, a member of the tribe of clerigos, was also a fine hearty don, who had no objection to a spree: whether in canonicals or not, he was particularly fond of cards, and he frequently employed the intervals between his religious duties on the sabbath in a rubber or two with others of his fraternity, who seemed much more expert in that way than in their exercise before their congregations.—Gambling is their favourite pastime, and they enjoy it more on Sundays than they do on any other day.

The chief employment here is carding and cleaning wool for the cloth manufactories. The females are constantly occupied in this business, assembled in groups at their doors and windows, picking the wool and getting it ready for the loom.

The men appear to be an idle, good for nothing race, lounging about the squares, or basking in the sun with their constant companion the cigar; here, or, when the weather is bad, round the brassiero, they congregate in knots, holding disputations on the politics of the day, a subject that is everlastingly on their tapis. In the evening the aristocracy of the place hold their Tertullias, which is a meeting where Dame Temperance presides. Collecting a pretty good number at the Caza of some comfortable Hidalgo, they carry on the old trade of gaming to some extent, the dons who do not play seating themselves with the senoras, a lively conversation is maintained, in which those damsels are by no means idle; nor do they in this, or any other sort of joint stock company, prove themselves to be sleeping partners. At those Tertullias there is no refreshing beverage stronger than the chrystal fluid, to wash down confectionary, or bolas (cakes), which are handed round on such occasions.

The French, whose head quarters were at Salamanca, twelve leagues from Bejar, had for some time previous to our arrival threatened to pillage this town and levy contributions on the inhabitants; but the British troops appearing, their plan was then disconcerted.—Finding, however, that one regiment alone was to compose the garrison, their former intentions were revived, and they accordingly prepared to make an immediate attack upon the place. The information we gained on this subject (as already noticed) was the means of keeping us on the alert, so that we were quite ready to give them a warm reception, whenever they might feel disposed to pay their long promised visit.

On the night of the 19th, when we were assembled with the civilians at their public ball-room, and were engaged in all the charming mazes of the dance, the harmony of our entertainment was interrupted by the appearance, *mal a-propos*, of one of the staff officials, armed *cap a pie*, and with lengthened visage. With matters of importance written on his brow, this harbinger of warlike tidings, looking like a descendant of him who "drew Priam's curtains in the dead of night," informed us that the enemy was rapidly advancing on the town, and that we must proceed, forthwith, to our respective stations at the wall.

Nothing could exceed the general confusion that immediately prevailed. Merriment and joyous glee were in a moment transformed to hurry and vexation. Waltzes and Boleros vanished like a dream, their place being taken by long faces and grim despair. The fair and lovely senoritas, who just now were all smiles, laughter and good-humour, became, in the twinkling of an eye, downcast, forlorn and woebegone. Like so many terrified rabbits, hunted from the warren, they ran screaming breathless and bonnetless in all directions, they knew not whither. The brilliant assemblage was soon dispersed, the scene being changed, as if by magic, into darkness, solitude and gloom.

Meanwhile, we, whose trade was bloodshed, war and battery, proceeded to our natural occupation, and, being already accoutred for the field, were quickly at the rendezvous, prepared for a little morning sport with the veterans in our front.

At an early hour General Foy, at the head of two thousand men, and a squadron of cavalry, was observed marching with hasty strides along the Salamanca road; and when it was clear day-light, their advanced guard, consisting of light troops, made a vigorous attack upon a strong picket of the 50th, commanded by Captain Benjamin Rowe, which had been posted at a farm house on the road.

Formidable by his numerical strength, the enemy pushed on regardless of all opposition, while the riflemen, stealing warily behind the rocks and broken ground, and concealed from our view by the surrounding mist and fog, penetrated almost to the very walls. With determined obstinacy the picket kept its station, disputing every inch, until at length, overpowered by superior numbers, it was compelled to fall back on the reserve, posted near the town.

Well armed parties of our men were drawn up at all the most exposed and assailable positions, and the utmost vigilance was required on their part to guard against surprise; the defences being so much extended, from their embracing the whole circuit of the scattered suburbs, that, had the French General made a bold and persevering assault, he must at least have gained access to the principal entrance of the place.

To this point Foy pushed forward with a considerable body of his troops, who, flushed by the success of their first onset, moved daringly forward, to force their way even to the principal street, and made a furious charge upon the party stationed at the gate. This small resolute band, detached from the main picket, was commanded by Lieutenant William Deighton, of the 50th grenadiers, who ranging his men across the passage, over which the archway was projected, resolved to defend to the utmost extremity the post at which he was stationed. Like a warrior of olden time this gallant soldier, of colossal build and stature, (for he was more than six feet high.) seemed as though he were himself able to check the further progress of the foe. His orders for the firing to commence, was answered by a peal so well directed, and with such deadly aim, as made the Frenchmen waver and fall back. A repetition of this warm salutation was answered by a sharp and rattling volley from the rifles of the Frenchmen; with bravery worthy of a better cause, the assailants still pressed on, closing after the soldiers under Rowe, until they arrived within thirty or forty paces of the walls.

Their spirit was, however, at length effectually damped by a repeated and destructive fire from our men, which sent them about like nine-pins, handling them so roughly, and finishing the morning's work by such an unmerciful *coup de grace*, that they could no longer hold their own. Having no power to rally, or withstand the treatment they met with, they collected the remnant of their scattered force, and forming into column, filed off with deliberate steps along the road, on which, puffed up by full assurance of success, they had so recently travelled.

They were soon after joined by the remainder of the troops under Foy, who, seeing that all further efforts would be in vain, marched off to his former quarters, chagrined in no small degree at his defeat, and no doubt regretting that he had ventured to attack a garrison composed of such tough materials.

The joy of the inhabitants of Bejar, on the departure of the enemy, could be only equalled by their gratitude; and, during the remainder of our stay among them, we were treated with a degree of kindness and hospitality, exceeding if possible all that we had hitherto experienced at their hands. Encouraged by these warm-hearted people, as well as by the smiles of beauty, we could not have felt any duty too severe, that might have been a means of protecting them from the rude embraces of Frenchmen, and from the plunder and destruction of their town and families.

CHAPTER XVII.

On the 17th of April, 1813, we marched from Bejar; I need not add that it was to the mutual regret of all parties; and, proceeding on the road leading to the Puerto de Banos, were cantoned that same night at the village of Banos near the pass.

In the early part of May, the several divisions of the English army broke up from their winter quarters, and, directing their course towards the northern provinces of Spain, commenced the last of the Peninsular Campaigns, namely, that celebrated one of 1813, during which the French were altogether expelled from the country, and the British standard was planted triumphantly on the Pyrenees.

On the 13th, the 2nd Division, under Lord Hill, moved forward. It was composed of the following regiments, the 28th, 29th, 31st, 34th, 39th, 50th, 57th, 66th, 71st and 92nd. Marching by successive routes, in the course of which, through the beautiful valley of the Ebro, we met with no extraordinary event to intercept our progress, we arrived, about the middle of June, on the plains of Vittoria.

At an early hour on the 21st of the month, the 1st Brigade, consisting of the 50th, 71st and, 92nd regiments passed through the town of La Puebla, and halted at its extremity on the main road: where, in consequence of intelligence received that morning, orders were given for the troops to hold themselves in readiness to meet the enemy in the course of the day.

Renewed life and animation possessed our men, on the assurance that an opportunity was at hand for giving the adverse party a specimen of their military skill, and likewise of escorting them safely across the Pyrenees. So unexpected, however, was the prospect of an immediate and warlike interview, that for some time the news was considered to be one of those false reports that are so often known to wing their flight about the line of march. But the tidings were soon confirmed by ocular demonstration; for on our rounding the head of a lofty promontory, that overhung an angle of the road, the French army was exposed to view, ready cut and dry, drawn up in order of battle, before Vittoria. Their several columns, formed in dark masses, contrasted with the green verdure of the surrounding fields, produced an effect resembling that of a closely planted forest, extending over the country in front of that town.

We had been travelling, for many days past, on short allowance, which, although it put us into excellent condition for a race, was by no means so favourable for a forward movement in the battle-field; moreover, there was nothing whatever forthcoming in the shape of provender, but, on the contrary, we ourselves were in a fair way of becoming food for gunpowder. To deteriorate still more our solitary situation, the commissary was not to be found; for, unfortunately, he either would not or could not keep up with us; and the consequence was, that we had no means of supply, a few loaves of dingy bread, sparingly served out, being the sole contents of our miserable breakfast. It was therefore evident that starvation as well as broken heads was to be the order of the day, and, should we escape the latter of these evils, the only chance to avoid the former was to rummage the first haversack we could find, for the contents of which the owner would most probably have no further occasion.

In this rueful state of things we again started, moving towards a chain of high mountains that bounded the western side of the valley. Having gained the termination of the level road, and arrived at the base of those heights, the brigade was again halted to obtain a little breathing time, as well as to take a look at the ammunition, examine the flints, and other preliminary measures usual in such cases.

During these proceedings, the 71st, commanded by Colonel Cadogan, pushed forward in double quick time; ascending the steep and rugged side of the hill, they penetrated through the wood by which it was covered, and, opening a brisk running fire right and left, dislodged the enemy's tirailleurs from every corner of their strong position. While advancing on this enterprise, the Highlanders suffered considerable loss, from the cool and deliberate aim of the French rifles; and their brave Colonel received a mortal wound. Being immediately conveyed to the summit of the eminence, he was informed of the successful career of our troops, and of the good conduct of his own followers, and soon after, with mild composure and tranquillity of mind, he resigned his gallant spirit without a murmur.

Cadogan, although a young man, was a most intelligent and experienced officer, and greatly valued by his noble relative Wellington, who placed so much confidence in his skill, and formed so high an opinion of his military talents, that on every occasion of importance he was entrusted with command.

The 50th and 92nd regiments, under the orders of Colonel Cameron of the latter, followed the example of the 71st, and marched onward by the steep circuitous route which that corps had traversed; and, after some delay as well as difficulty in clearing through the heath and brushwood that overspread the pathway, succeeded at length in attaining the highest part of the eminence, from whence, after forming into column, they continued to advance along the edge of the precipice.

On this elevation, raised far above the plain on which the hostile armies were contending, we had almost a bird's eye view of the whole field of action, spread out, as it were, like a map beneath our feet. The reverberation of the artillery among the rocks, by which we were surrounded, the echo of the continued rolling of musketry, the confused noise and din of the battle's turmoil, the varied bright and polished arms, accoutrements, and trappings of the combatants, as they shone resplendent in the rays of a brilliant sun,—the rapid movements of the Cavalry to and fro,—the manœuvring of the infantry, together with an endless variety of circumstances connected with the pomp of war, formed on the whole a scene of awful grandeur, unrivalled by any thing that the imagination of man could fancy.

The enemy, meanwhile, made considerable resistance, while slowly retiring from hill to hill, and his light troops, taking advantage of every means of cover, tormented us exceedingly, and picked off a number of our best men and officers. The 71st continued in advance, and crossed that part of the mountain which was scooped out on one side into a deep ravine or hollow, where, gaining the extreme point of a high and broken promontory, they took firm lodgment in a position, the rocks almost seeming to be formed by the hand of nature into a fortress of great strength. In this situation they were observed by a numerous party of the French, who were posted near them, on some commanding ground, and whom, from their dress and appearance, they mistook for Spanish troops. Finding this would do for a very good *ruse de guerre,* the treacherous deceit was kept up, and, as soon as the Highlanders had assembled within range, the enemy opened a raking and murderous volley upon their ranks; and so desperately did they maintain this fire, that, in a little time, the gallant 71st was almost cut to pieces without being able to return a single shot. Being compelled to retire across the ravine, the remainder of the regiment fell back on the brigade.

On our march across this ground, an incident occurred which made a deep impression on the minds of those who happened to be present at the time. Across the pathway, and on either side, men and officers were lying, and one of the latter was extended on his face among the heath and brushwood, so close to where we passed, that Major Malcolm Mackenzie of the 70th, prompted as it were by intuition, suddenly dismounted to ascertain who was the individual. Stooping to observe the features, that were partly concealed by the long broom, he started back with grief and consternation, on perceiving that the young soldier, who had thus fallen an early victim, was his brother, Lieutenant Colin Mackenzie of the same regiment.

The gallant Major, thus taken by surprise, was so much affected by the event that it was a considerable time before he recovered from the melancholy shock. He was himself killed in France, in the course of a few months, after having run an honourable career throughout the whole of the Peninsular war. They were both sons of Captain H. Mackenzie, the Paymaster of the regiment, who was highly esteemed and respected by the 71st, in which he had served many years.

The whole line moving forward along the ridge, the entire extent of which by this time was carried, our troops followed the retiring enemy with steady perseverance, until all opposition having ceased throughout the field, a general halt took place, and the firing was discontinued.

The fugitives, in straggling bodies, fled precipitately towards the woods, through which the road to Salvatierra leads; their numbers being every moment swelled, and their confusion rendered irretrievable, by fresh accessions from Vittoria and other quarters, myriads of the routed foe covered the distant country as far as the eye could reach, their route being traceable by a continuous and lengthened train of baggage, guns, and wounded, as well as by the interminable multitude of followers, that are always to be found upon the skirts of a beaten, or in fact of any other, army. Of prisoners taken the number was consequently great, and the whole of the baggage and artillery fell into our hands together with most of the wounded.*

* While employed in some hot work upon the hill, I observed an instance of "taking things coolly," even in the midst of fire, which is worthy of noticing here.

One of our Captains, a brave, intrepid soldier from the other

We bivouacked in the woods to the North of Vittoria that night, in a condition quite enough to cool the military ardour of the most ambitious warriors; reduced to the borders of utter famine, and harassed by continued exertion. The successful issue of this day's operations acted, however, as a balm for all our troubles, and although it furnished not our humble board, was nevertheless a means of encouragement, which served to banish the desponding thoughts that, under other circumstances, might have weighed us down.

---

side of the Tweed, (who had been so often in the smoke that he seemed only in his proper element when the balls were whizzing past his grisly locks, and the music of great guns was sounding in his ears,) happened to get a crack in the arm, of so violent a nature as to fracture the bone. Regardless of the wound, while the blood was streaming fast, he looked down sorrowfully on the damage effected on his precious garment, the object of his tenderest care, which had so often been wheeled to the right about, that with respect to it, the old adage of "one good turn deserves another" was virtually attended to, and, after eyeing wistfully the awful breach, with greater horror than he would the breach of Badajos, or any other he was about to storm, he cast an angry glance towards that quarter from whence the missile was sent, and exclaimed, in none of the softest tones, as though he wished the whole French army might hear his voice, "Dom the fellows, they've spoiled my cott!"

The casualties in the 1st brigade were not of great extent, compared with those of others in the field. Our business was chiefly on the heights; we were therefore not so much exposed to the fire of cannon as those who were engaged upon the plain. The light troops bore the heat and burthen of the day, getting the hardest knocks, while the battalions acting in support and in reserve, were much more gently dealt with.

CHAPTER XVIII.

On the 22nd of June, we pursued our journey on the road by which the fragments of Jourdan's army had retreated, and, passing through Salvatierra and other towns, we arrived before Pampeluna, early in July. Soon after this we entered the valley of Bastan, situated on the boundaries of the Lower Pyrenees.

While we were advancing towards the Pyrenees, a most tremendous storm burst upon the column, as it was marching over the crest of a lofty ridge. The thunder rolled in fearful peals, and the forked lightning, attracted by the polished fire-arms and bayonet points, flashed about our heads in an awful manner, threatening destruction to the troops. Lieut. Masterman of the 34th was struck by the electric fluid, with such fatal violence that his death was instantaneous; his features scorched and blackened, and his body burnt almost to a cinder, presented a frightful spectacle as he lay extended on the road.

Here commenced that system of manœuvring on the enemy's flanks, by which, day after day, we forced him to retire from the commanding ground where he had been posted. Instead of running directly into the lion's mouth, we paid our respects in a more cautious manner. The light troops were dispatched, and, taking a widely extended circuit right and left, closed in upon the wings of the adverse party, threatening their communication with the rear. The French, instead of making any resistance in these wild and thickly wooded glens, adopted a more prudent line of conduct, and, not having any particular appetite for cold steel, scampered off to the next range of heights at the moment when we expected to have had a brush, leaving us, by way of a legacy, their half extinguished fires, their broken huts, and all the rubbish of a deserted camp.

Agreeable to this novel mode of tactics, which was the standing, or rather the chacing, order of the day, our divisions proceeded onward, the advanced guard of each leading into a difficult country, the roads winding through vast chasms and narrow defiles, by which the lower branches of the Pyrenean chain are intersected.

As we approached the more lofty range, we passed through Lanz, Erruita, Elisonda, and other clean and well inhabited places, our route still penetrating through deep ravines, and bending with the sinuous current of the Upper Bidassoa river, by which the verdant fields and pasture lands are fertilized.

The whole extent of the vale of Bastan presents, on every side, the most beautiful scenery that can be imagined. The green and richly cultivated meadows, as contrasted with the naked and inaccessible heights by which they are surrounded, produce an effect that renders the appearance of the landscape at once impressive and delightful. The lover of nature in its varied and romantic forms might here enjoy a prospect, of which it would be impossible by words to convey even a limited idea.

On the 8th of July, 1813, the 1st Brigade of the 2nd Division, marched into Elisonda, and, proceeding forward for about a league, halted on the brow of an elevated ridge, from the summit of which the ground descended in a slope, thinly covered with woods, to the extremity of our position.

The 71st and 92nd were encamped on the main passes of the mountain, to the left of the Bayonne road; and the 50th was bivouacked among some trees, about a mile to the right of the corps. The enemy at this period having been driven from all the roads leading across the Pyrenees, came to a stand on a range of strong hills, commanding the principal approaches into France.

Marshal Soult, their general in chief, disappointed and mortified at thus being defeated and expelled from the Peninsula, determined to make one last and desperate effort to regain a footing in that country; he therefore made preparations for a grand attack upon our lines, and put his threat in execution on the 25th of the month. The heights, in every direction, were covered by the French encampments, in which we could discern large bodies of their troops assembling.

About this time, while we were in the enjoyment of our bivouac and the invigorating influence of the mountain air, an amusing scene took place in the lines of the 50th. In the middle of one of the dark nights, during our station on the hill, a dreadful storm came on, upsetting huts, wigwams, and all the paraphernalia of our camp. During the commotion, the mules and other baggage animals, terrified by the howling of the wind, broke loose from their moorings, took flight in every direction, and getting entangled among the tent cords they cast us all adrift. Bewildered amidst the gloom, and dreaming of war's alarms, it seemed as though the French were in among us, or that a caravan of wild beasts was set at liberty. Such bellowing, screams and shouting from right to left, at once resounded throughout the hill, that the storm was quiet in comparison. Drums and bugles giving the alarm, accompanied by the braying of a hundred jack-asses, with the clamorous tongues of men, women and dogs, combined to produce an opera, or rather, a tragi-comedy, of so ludicrous a nature as was never witnessed on the Pyrenees before.—In a state of demi-nudity, (finding that no tangible enemy was in the field,) each returned to the wreck of his shattered dormitory, where, endeavouring to crouch beneath the well-drenched canvass, or the more wretched shelter of the trees, we lay in torpid misery, waiting patiently the return of day.

The morning of the 25th of July was ushered in by a bright sun, and other favourable appearances, denoting the continuance of fine weather. About noon intelligence came that the enemy was advancing in strong force upon the pickets; in a few minutes the whole of our line was formed, and the 50th, 71st and 92nd drew up on the highest part of the ridge.—From thence were perceived large bodies, covered by a host of light troops, rapidly driving in our outposts. The pickets, together with the 34th regiment, under the command of Colonel Fenwick, of that corps, immediately occupied some elevated rocks, on the right of our position. Soult, observing with his experienced eye that this important post was not sufficiently strengthened, sent a number of his men to dislodge our soldiers from the spot.—After a sharp and sanguinary contest, (Colonel Fenwick being severely wounded,) our troops descended from the hill, and fell back with considerable loss upon the brigade. By this time the French in solid masses were gaining fast the steep sides of the mountain, preceded by a swarm of riflemen, clambering the ascent like wild cats, and rushing on with incredible gallantry towards the summit, in order to gain a lodgment there. Having accomplished this, and the whole extent of our line being under the range of fire, we were exposed to a most destructive shower; the balls whistling past our ears, like hail stones driven in a storm, tumbled our men in every direction. Resistance now was unavailing against such odds, and, although an incessant peal of musketry was opened on the enemy, our situation was no longer tenable, and we retired upon the next height, leaving many killed and wounded on the ground.*

Our right wing suffered greatly on this occasion, most of the grenadiers were cut off, and their leader, Captain William Ambrose, was mortally wounded in the groin; among the slain was likewise Lieutenant William Deighton, of the same company, a native of Cumberland, who so gallantly defended his post at the gates of Bejar, and whose conduct at all times was that of a cool and intrepid soldier.

Ensigns Williams and White were also killed

* Colonel Fenwick was, on his return to England, appointed Governor of Pendennis Castle, where he died a few years since from the consequences of his wound.

—the former carried the King's Colours, which falling with him, another officer, who observed the circumstance, conveyed them to a place of safety; Williams was a young officer who volunteered with men from the Warwickshire militia, and had scarcely recovered from a wound received at Vittoria—White had been for many years our Quarter Master Sergeant, and in consequence of his merit, he had lately been promoted in the regiment; he was a man advanced in life, and an excellent worthy character, esteemed by us all.

The conduct of Lieutenant Charles Brown of the light company was conspicuous; seeing the Frenchmen pressing closely in, he was determined to lend a hand in giving them a check, in a manner which he could not accomplish with the feeble weapon which he wielded; he therefore seized a musket, (plenty of which were scattered about), and extending himself upon a bank of earth, let fly with such deliberate aim, that many of the Frenchmen were effectually stopped in their career. Brown was an excellent shot, and enjoyed the thing amazingly, appearing quite in his element, going about his work as methodically as if he were shooting partridges or wild ducks, shewing a degree of skill worthy of the most practised amateur.

This was the only instance of the kind that ever came within my observation, and can be justified only by the strong desire a sportsman, (for he was a zealous son of Nimrod), had to indulge his ruling passion; for officers, in general, have too much to attend to, while in action, and therefore could not, were they so inclined, indulge their fancy in that way.

The Lieutenant joined us from the East Middlesex militia, from which he brought a number of volunteers. He was an active good-looking fellow, and a most agreeable companion. He was afterwards severely wounded, and retired on half-pay to enjoy a pension which he very deservedly obtained. Having once more to abandon our position, the 50th and 39th fell back upon that on which the 92nd was drawn up. O'Callaghan, amidst the din of arms, calling to his soldiers with the tones of a Stentor, "steady 39th ordinary time!" these corps actually retired with the most deliberate pace, as if upon parade.

The Highlanders under Cameron, stood firm, and maintained their post with determined bravery until their ammunition was expended, when, borne down by legions, the remnant of these devoted Northerns withdrew to the contiguous hill.—Their Colonel, having had two horses shot under him, and being twice severely wounded, was forced to quit the field.* Captain Bevan, of the 92nd Grenadiers, was wounded at the same time, as well as many other officers of that corps.

When the 50th was again formed on the hill to which they had retired, they were supported by the 39th, with the Hon. Colonel O'Callaghan at their head. Both these corps poured in a tremendous volley from right and left, while O'Callaghan, a stern Hibernian, by

* Colonel Cameron commanded the 92nd, throughout the whole Peninsular war, with honor to himself and to his regiment. He fell nobly, at Quatre Bras, in the centre of a square which was formed to repel a strong body of French cavalry.

his own example, stimulated his men to personal acts of valour.

The enemy, meanwhile, nothing daunted by this destructive fire, pushed forward with renewed exertion, urged on by the spirited exhortations and conduct of their officers. The latter with signal courage took the lead, and waved caps or cloaks with one hand, while with the other they brandished their sabres in the air, shouting out—"Vive L'Empereur! en avant! mes enfans!" Thus gallantly headed and additionally animated, drums beating and trumpets sounding, the columns rushed on with wild and desperate fury.

While the 50th was acting in support of the 92nd, Colonel Charles Hill of the former was struck in the groin by a spent ball; and had scarcely recovered from the shock, when another hit him on the forehead, which caused him at once to fall, to all appearance mortally wounded, and with deep concern his soldiers beheld him carried off the field; the command devolving on Major Thomas Dundass Campbell.

The increasing masses of the enemy bore down all before them; and the 50th and 92nd, the latter then commanded by Major Mitchell, retiring from hill to hill, defending with obstinate resistance every inch of ground, halted about five o'clock in the evening on the brow of a lofty and precipitous rock, the highest point of the lower Pyrenees, and to the left of the pass of Maya. The 71st, whose encampment we had crossed, suffered considerably while covering this movement, and was at length compelled to join the rest of the Brigade.

Elated by the issue of their formidable attacks, our adversaries persevered in the arduous struggle, to gain the passes, and, although at the expence of considerable numbers, still kept possession of every piece of ground by which those passes were commanded. Their riflemen, with unparalleled boldness ferretting their way within less than pistol shot of where we stood, by a rambling fire did very great execution throughout our already diminished ranks. With such precision did those experienced artists do their duty that very many of our companions were killed or wounded on this height. A party of the officers of the 50th, who were collected in a knot, discussing the affairs of the eventful day, were quickly seen by those marksmen, who, from behind the rocks, dispatched with deadly aim a few rifle missiles, each with its billet; and the balls were so faithful to their errand that the congress was soon dissolved, some of the members being sent to "that bourne from which no traveller returns," and the remainder wounded. Among those who fell on this occasion, was Lieutenant Hugh Birchall of the 4th battalion company, which he had commanded for some time. Having fallen ill, he was in his bed at Elisonda, when the battle commenced, and hearing the noise of musketry, he thought that something was going forward in the lines, in which he ought to bear a part. With a mind endued with strength superior to that of his weakly frame, he arose from the couch of sickness, and calling all the vigour that he could muster to his aid, tottered with feeble pace to the field of action, arriving at a late hour upon the hill. Exhausted, pale, and like one risen from the dead, he resumed his former place, and scarcely had he joined the group assembled in the front, when, by a fatal bullet, this spirited young man was numbered with the slain.

In crossing the place where the 71st had been encamped, a party of the enemy pitched a tent belonging to that corps, and, forming in a ring about this trophy, made the hills echo with their shouts of triumph.

The 82nd and other regiments coming up at that period soon obliged them to change the notes of their song, and put an effectual damper on their pastime. The Brigade of General Barnes and some German troops, arriving opportunely to support the 82nd, made a desperate charge upon them, and following up this bold attack drove them completely across the pass, and back to the ground where they had been posted.—No further efforts were made on their part to renew the contest.—Had there been sufficient time the 7th division would have totally expelled them from the mountains, but daylight failing brought to a conclusion one of the most sanguinary and hard fought battles recorded in the annals of the Peninsular war.

The 50th lost a considerable number of men in this action; and the following officers were among the killed and wounded: *killed*—Captain Wm. Ambrose, Lieutenant W. Deighton, Grenadiers, Ensign Williams, Ensign White: *wounded*—Lieutenant Colonel C. Hill,* Captain Charles Grant, Light Company; Roger North, Lieutenants McDonald, Patterson, Nowlan and Jones; Ensigns Collins and Bateman.

In consequence of the right of the line at Roncesvalles having been carried by a superior force, and also by reason of the loss sustained, the 2nd and 7th divisions, cooperating with the rest of the army, retired on the night of

* It was at first supposed that Colonel Hill was killed, and he was returned on that list, but after a most singular recovery, he was able to join the regiment previous to their embarkation for England. Captain Grant had his leg amputated, but continued in full pay. Lieutenant McDonald was afterwards killed at Aire, in France.

the 25th, and morning of the 26th of July, and after passing along the road that leads through the Valley of Bastan, they formed on the hills in front of Erruita. Here the British made a determined stand, beat the enemy back, and followed up the blow with so much vigour that he was completely routed, driven through all the passes, and forced once more to take refuge in his own country.

CHAPTER XIX.

The writer of this narrative being wounded, he joined the long train of maimed and mutilated aspirants for honour and glory, who wended their way slowly and with painful steps to the City of Vittoria, where the principal hospital stations for the army were established. The cavalcade was not of that description which will excite any pleasurable emotions in the mind; those of despondency were the most prevailing, which the departure from our brother soldiers was not in any degree calculated to diminish. However, this being all the "fortune of war," we jogged along patiently, some on mules, others on waggons, and not a few on the humble jackass, forming on the whole a procession of so motley and varied a character that, by the time we reached our journey's end, we were not unlike Sir John Falstaff's recruits, with whom he was ashamed to enter Coventry. We cut a most interesting appearance, some with heads tied up, and some with limbs, as we made our entré at a funereal pace, exhausted and chopfallen, loaded with as plentiful a supply of *fame* as the most zealous amateur cou.d desire. Nothing could exceed the anxiety depicted in the countenances of those who had been in Vittoria, since the battle there. So many vague reports had been circulated with regard to the army, that they were unacquainted with the true state of things, and hastened to meet the travellers, as they approached the town, and with deeply interested looks enquired the fate of their brave companions in the field. Accompanied by our friends, who kindly sympathized with us, each of us repaired to his proper quarters.

Mine were at the house of a respectable looking man, who, though a Spaniard, proved by his manner and conduct that in his heart he was a Frenchman. To his spouse, a dame not unworthy of so treacherous a helpmate, our application for any means of comfort or accommodation was of no avail, and beyond the luxury of a hard mattress, upon a harder floor, with bare walls to look at, neither I, nor any of the luckless cavaliers that were billetted under the roof of these inhospitable people, could obtain any thing whatever.

Los Franceses were the favourites; and as for the English, our patron would have rejoiced at their expulsion from the country. Doubtless, this partisan held a different style of language, when he was informed, that his very particular friends were completely ousted from every part of Spain. In a front room of this mansion, the occupant was Lieut. Alexander H. Pattison of the 74th regiment, who was severely wounded at Vittoria, and whose society and conversation contributed greatly to relieve the tedium of our solitary lodging. Pattison was above seven years eldest lieutenant in the 74th, and became, in the course of time, Lieut. Colonel of the 2nd West India Regiment, in the command of which he died at the Bahamas.

Captain Gough, of the 68th, was quartered in the next house, where we passed some pleasant days, while comparing notes on the subject of our late adventures. Poor Gough I never saw again. He was a passenger from America, (where his regiment was quartered), in the Union Packet, which was shipwrecked off the coast of Ireland, and was among those who unfortunately perished.

Vittoria is a well built and populous city, with regular streets, and a handsome Square. The country around is abundant in all the productions of so fine a climate, and did not seem to have experienced any of those evils incident to war. The inhabitants in general treated the British officers with civility, but many were inwardly our enemies. Some time after our arrival, however, they thought it better policy to affect a degree of reverence for us, and make wondrous professions, of the sincerity of which we had certain doubts.

It was during our stay here, that the Honorable Captain Gore, of the 94th regiment, was put to death by a party sent to force an entrance into his quarters, in order to convey from thence a lovely and interesting damsel, whom that officer had taken under his protection. Of this tragical event there has been so many different versions, that, if I were to relate the particulars as reported at the time, the account would probably vary from others that were published. I shall therefore forbear from any detail of the painful and melancholy narrative. The gallant Captain was certainly imprudent in resisting the Spanish authorities. Knowing as he did the prejudices of the country, the results of the illfated attachment might have easily been foreseen; for, thus to get involved so seriously with a fair Senorita could not fail to exasperate and excite the vengeance of her family.—The unfortunate affair was truly to be deplored on every account. Gore was a fine promising young man, and his inamorata (since entombed within a convent), was beautiful.

The good people of Vittoria enjoyed themselves, while we remained, as much as any other set of mortals in this transitory state of being. Apparently indifferent as to what might become of their politics, they assembled, during the cool and refreshing hours of evening, in groups around the doors, making merry among each other with lively chattering, and peals of laughter, that flew, in a sort of running fire, from one end of the city to the other.

About this time, the celebration of a grand festival, in honour of one of their numerous saints, was going forward. During its continuance, the place was in a state of noisy uproar, and the people were infected with a sort of dancing mania, enough to gladden the heart of St. Vitus himself. We were insufferably tormented with the unmerciful squealing of fifes, and upon the parchment they were perpetually drumming in our ears.

Between the hours of feasting, the townspeople, of all ranks and ages, sallied from their dwellings; old and young, rich and poor, were on the pavé, from the child in leading strings, to the wrinkled hag of eighty, all afflicted with the mania. On a signal for a general ballet, and the music striking up, the crazy multitude, electrified in every limb, commenced an exhibition of gymnastics unequalled by the most skilful artist, sufficient to make even an anchorite grin and stare. It was quite amusing to see the aged spinster, whose charms were faded by the hand of time, with pinioned elbows, tripping it with an antiquated beau; the withered grandame hobbling on her feeble pins to some venerable don; and the smirking lass with amorous eye, and attitudes enticing, figuring away with a gallant cavaleiro. It was, in short, a most ridiculous display of asses in human form. The Shakers of America, or the dancing Dervishes of Turkey, were in comparison tame. Pushing, jostling, screaming, and ogling, seemed to be all the mode throughout the motley crowd, so that were a stranger suddenly to make his appearance, he would fancy that the inmates of some lunatic asylum had been liberated, and were playing off their antics through the town. Ever and anon, some would retire within their doors, but other fools supplied their place, and in single ranks arrayed on either side the street, like those drawn up in a country dance, they exhibited in a style that Vestris might have wondered at.

There was a curious medley of mirth and sadness throughout the city, which to the sufferer and the invalid was but a mockery of his woes. Quietness and peace would have been far more grateful than such illtimed, unwelcome and vociferous revels.

Early in September, 1813, accompanied by Lieutenant Rhodes, of the 39th regiment, I set out from Vittoria, on the route to Bilboa, for the purpose of embarking for England. Proceeding towards the northern Provinces, we arrived at Tolosa on the following day, where we remained one night. The landlord of the posada at which we brought up, was a very humorous character, and also an extremely odd fish; but he was one who had an eye to business, taking good care of the main chance, for, hearing of the success of the British arms, and that some of the troops were likely to pass that way, he fitted up his hotel in good style, and went to such expense, that it would have been a pity had he been disappointed. With regard to the exterior of his premises, he was determined to make a display of his loyalty, and therefore put up the sign of Fernando Settimo, whose ugly countenance was no great attraction to the traveller. By his conversation, in a sort of mongrel Anglo-Spanish dialect, one would suppose that he was a veritable patriot, and that he reverenced the English. The inscription on his signboard, however, seemed to put a different face on the matter; for by his own shewing it would appear that upon the thick skull of this worthy the organ of destructiveness was strongly marked, or, in other words, that he was neither more nor less than a cannibal. The passenger, therefore, might well start with horror, on perusing the aforesaid notice, which by the arrangement of the painter, ran thus:

"FRANCISCO PEREZ, ESTALAGEM

FOR EATING

GENTLEMEN LODGED WITHIN."

Poor Francisco was evidently not in the schoolmaster's line of march; for in his attempt at an English sign, by not minding his own *stops*, he publickly forewarned all who might be journeying that way, that *their stops* in this world should not be of long duration. Giving nevertheless this honest Spaniard full credit for all his promises of civility, and having no particular dread of being hashed up into minced meat, or an olla-podrida, we lodged ourselves in his hostelry, happy, after a long and fatiguing march, to get a place of rest, even under such inauspicious circumstances.

We arrived at Bilboa in a few days, having had rather a pleasant though protracted journey. Rhodes being a good travelling companion, we got on smoothly enough, with a certain independance of character very much to be envied; for as we were entirely out of the range of adjutants, orderly books, and other such unfashionable concerns, we felt like gentlemen at large, with light hearts, and, not being overburdened with cash, with still lighter pockets. As to our worldly goods and chattels, we might apply to ourselves Jack's favourite ditty.

> " A handkerchief held all the treasure I had,
> Which over my shoulder I threw," &c.

We found at Bilboa much kindness and hospitality, and were lodged in quarters that a prime minister might have envied. Like other large communities, the place had a lively and social aspect, which appearance was considerably improved by fresh importations of John Newcomes from England, in search of laurels and broken pates, as well as hard goers from the army, with their brows already crowned, but minus in the usual complement of legs and arms. The weather proved unfavourable, and prevented our seeing the lions of the place, but, as those are not generally numerous or curious in the Spanish towns, our loss was nothing to grieve about, nor do I think that, had we seen them, the description would have been either amusing or edifying.

On the 29th of September, we entered the small sea-port of Passages, having, in our route from Bilboa, lodged in several good looking places. After concluding every arrangement with regard to our affairs, we embarked on the 5th of October, in a small brig, bound for Plymouth, taking final leave of a country where, for so long a period, we had been engaged in all varieties of campaigning, and where, amidst the toils and dangers of our wandering life, we experienced some happy days, with so much of unmingled pleasure, that, although we were proceeding homeward to our beloved native land, more of sadness than of joy was felt when parting from the shore.

Before we got out into the open sea, we sailed through an intricate and narrow passage, which seemed, as it were, a natural fissure of tremendous depth, violently rent asunder, by earthquake or volcanic agency, through the steep and precipitous mountain ridge by which this part of the coast is bound. The scenery, in the midst of the close and dangerous channel, was of a desolate character. There was no apparent means of egress from the dark and gloomy chasm, walled in on either side by huge rocks, rising far above the topmast head, and the hazardous attempt to steer a vessel through in stormy weather, would prove fatal to those who might rashly undertake the perilous navigation.

Our voyage across the Bay of Biscay was unattended with any thing remarkable or uncommon, and was in every way as favourable as could be wished. In about five days we landed at Plymouth, rejoicing at the idea of being once more on the shores of Britain.

CHAPTER XX.

ALTHOUGH I was unfortunately deprived of knowing by personal observation the movements of the 50th, I have, however, good authority for stating an outline of their proceedings. Fighting their way as usual, they were present in everything that was going on during the ensuing campaign, and, after lending a hand in drumming the enemy out of the Pyrenees, they carried the British colours into France, where they performed a very distinguished part, at the passage of the Nive and the Adour. They were also shortly engaged at Orthes, Tarbes, Aire, and other places; in short, whenever there was anything to be done in this line of business, the old boys were sure to be in the thick of it.

While they were advancing to the attack, at Aire, the pickets were in front, skirmishing with the French light troops, covered by a deep ditch, or breast-work, above which the instant one of our party attempted to shew his head, he was without ceremony popped off. This sort of wholesale slaying was too much of a good thing, and kindled up the wrath of Lieutenant Duncan McDonald, a fiery little North-Briton, who, getting rather impatient and fidgety, called on his men to follow him, in order to have a dash at those fellows, who were thus making their comrades food for crows. As he was jumping across the top of the ditch into the field, and before a single man had time to join him, he was struck by a rifle ball, and fell dead upon the spot. The soldiers, immediately rushing forward, took ample vengeance for the loss we had sustained, and charged the marksmen with such effect that they took to flight in all directions, evacuating entirely the town and neighbourhood.

In the absence of Colonel Hill, Brevet Lieutenant Colonel Harrison commanded the 50th, and on every occasion the gallantry of this officer was conspicuous, and it is remarkable, that in the midst of all that fighting he never received the slightest wound.

Brevet Major W. A. Gordon, 50th, was entrusted with the command of the advance battalions in forcing the passage of the Nive, and for his bravery and intrepid conduct on that service he was promoted to the rank of Lieutenant Colonel.

Among those who fell dangerously wounded on the advance to Bayonne, was Captain Robert Verney Lovett;—he died in England, in consequence of the injury he received, and being a man of social and convivial qualities he was much regretted.

The following officers of the 50th were killed, wounded, or taken prisoners, from the battles in the Pyrenees to the termination of the war in France: *killed*—Lieutenant and Adjutant William Myles; Lieutenant and Adjutant Duncan McDonald—*wounded*—Captain H. Custance, Captain R. V. Lovett; Lieutenant R. Keddle; Ensign Sawkings—*missing*—Lieutenant General Bartley—*prisoner* Lieutenant General Power.*

In the course of these campaigns, I had many opportunities of estimating the comparative merits of English, Scotch and Irish soldiers, of which there has been a good deal said, and on which there is so much difference of opinion, that it seems difficult to arrive at any truth upon the subject. Military men alone can form any idea of what those soldiers can accomplish. For my part, I believe, that in one essential point, that is, with regard to courage, there is not the slightest shade of difference; at least I never could observe any, the men of

* Myles was wounded in the ancle, but died soon after of locked jaw; he was an active and zealous officer, and a quiet inoffensive man. Duncan McDonald was killed at Aire. Keddle died in Enniskillen. Power on half-pay. Custance is now Lieutenant Colonel, commanding the 9th Regiment. Sawkins, leg amputated. Lovett died in England. Bartley, Pay Master 50th, in New South Wales.

each nation showing themselves possessed of a pretty equal share of the commodity in question, or what is usually called mettle. It is merely as to temper and disposition, in particular situations, that they may sometimes vary.

Simply speaking, were it necessary to employ a body of troops upon a service where they might be much exposed to fire, or which required a great degree of cool and steady firmness to effect the object of their Chief, while at the same time they were to be engaged with an obstinate foe, and that for a continuance, I should certainly select the Englishman, who performs his duty well, because he knows of nothing but obedience. There is, in general, no particularly actuating principal in him but this. With reference to his friends and country, John Bull hardly ever thinks upon the subject; he is not a very meditative animal, but pursues his straight forward course without flinching, and with a zealous desire to acquire the good opinion of his officers immediately around him, whose example he will follow even to the breach. In quarters there are none more easily managed, and as for good order and cleanliness of person, they surpass the soldiers of every country. They likewise display much of personal vigour, being strong, athletic and well-formed, so that when a charge is to be made, the bayonet in their hands becomes a most dangerous weapon, the effect of which has been severely felt by their enemies in every corner of the globe.

Were I at liberty to choose a party upon whose steadiness in camp and quarters, and upon whose fidelity to orders, I might depend, and who, from love of country, take pride in the most implicit obedience to their officers, even while suffering all the miseries of hard service, cold and famine, commend me to the Scotch. Their esprit de corps, and faithful attachment to their chiefs and clans, is proverbial, and form the actuating powers of influence with them, prompting them to follow their leaders, even "to the cannon's mouth," while the pibroch is ringing in their ears. Talk to a Highlander of his heaths and mountains, and remind him of his honour, his blood gets up, and he will burn with ardour to signalize himself for the honour of his people. To learn the character of the Scotch regiments, look to the page of history.

Now for the Hibernian—Come along, my lads,! hurrah!—They may well be called rough and ready fellows; not over solicitous about personal appearance, they use no unnecessary delay about the toilet, and are therefore always at hand, and prepared for a start, at any moment or on any duty, when their services may be wanted. Is there a fort to be stormed, or a castle wall to be escaladed, then, they are the boys for your work. Only let them have a little word of encouragement, accompanied, (if you like), with a small drop "just to keep the could out of their stomachs," by way of priming, and they will assault a battery bristled with cannon. As for behaviour in quarters, they are now and then a little unruly to be sure, for Pat, when he gets a taste of the creatur, is rather a pugnacious being. The Irishmen are, however, firm soldiers in the field, and nothing can match them in the bivouac, where their fertile genius comes into play; while the veterans of other corps are gazing about them, they have got their huts made, their wood cut, and may be seen scampering all over the country, in search of all the good things that may be had for love or money—

> " Pat is the fellow that lives on his pay,
> And spends half a crown out of sixpence a-day."

The 3rd division, (Sir Thomas Picton's), was called the fighting division. It was chiefly composed of Irishmen. This is quite as much as if volumes were written on the subject. Look to the 87th at Barrosa, the 88th at Badajos, the 27th and 45th every where.

More need not be said.

The German troops are superior to any I ever met with for strict attention to duty. They are determined, brave, and cool in the hour of battle; and, should they be entrusted with the out-posts, the camp may sleep in safety, and in full assurance of being vigilantly watched.—Hardy and inflexible, they conform under any state of things to their commanders, at whose will they move with the regularity of a piece of mechanism.

There was a company of the 60th rifles attached to our Brigade, who were all Germans. They were commanded by Captain Philip Blassiere, a singularly active and zealous officer. Throughout the whole period of our warfare he never was absent from his station. With unwearied perseverance he braved the hardest weather and the roughest service; his athletic frame and iron constitution enabling him to withstand it all, holding out with stubborn tenacity while hundreds gave way around him. Undergoing all hardships in common with his men, he walked by their side, partook of the same fare, and shared not only with them the dangerous trade of fighting, but all the miseries of cold and famine with their attendant train of horrors. He was foremost on all occasions, where shot and shell abounded, and was at the rendezvous before a man of the brigade was assembled; and long before the march commenced, there was Blassiere ready with his Germans for any thing that might be wanted.

The external appearance of this man was well calculated to excite surprise, and corresponded with his character for self-denial. His wardrobe was of the most scanty nature; the jacket and other parts of his attire, the original colour of which could not be distinguished by the most microscopic eye, were worn out, patched, and threadbare, and were pieced in various places; and the whole of his costume seemed at least for the last seven years to have retained its original situation on the person of its owner. Thus accoutred he trudged along, indifferent about the elements; as fast as he got wet, he got dry again, for he never changed his clothes. His muscular neck was enclosed by a hard leather stock and brass clasp to match, and all his trappings were of the same coarse materials as those worn by his men. The haversack, manufactured of rough canvass, sometimes proved a treacherous friend, for through many rents and breaches, made by the hand of time, the mouldy and crumbling biscuit found its way, leaving but the fragments of his bare allowance. The blue canteen, well clasped with iron hoops, afforded him a source of comfort; its contents being to him a certain panacea for all evils.

With habits somewhat eccentric, he was never known to indulge in any thing beyond the rations; and having no desire for the society of others, he discussed his frugal meal in solitude, avoiding even the luxury of a tent. His good humoured though weatherbeaten countenance was the index of his mind, which was cheerful and contented.

After buffetting all the storms, roughing it through thick and thin, and standing out the pelting of many a shower of bullets, this gallant veteran fell at last in battle when the army entered France.

CHAPTER XXI.

Intelligence being received that peace was concluded, the second Division of the Army embarked at Bordeaux, and, sailing from the Garonne, arrived in England early in 1814. The 50th was ordered to Cork, and, after marching through various parts of the Emerald Isle, they were sent to the north of it, where with the head quarters in Aughnacloy, they remained for the winter of the same year. Early in the spring of 1815, the regiment was removed to Enniskillen.* Here we were treated with the most liberal hospitality, not only by the inhabitants of the town, but by those of the surrounding neighbourhood, who generously received and entertained the officers, during the whole time of our residence there. The 2nd Battalion of the 27th, and some troops of the 7th Dragoon Guards, together with the staff of the Fermanagh Militia, composed the garrison, the whole in charge of Major General Stephen Mahon.

Bonaparte's return from Elba was the signal for renewed warlike preparations: hence every possible means were resorted to for the augmentation of the British Army. The troops in Enniskillen commenced beating up with active zeal, and our regiment having on its return from France been reduced to a mere skeleton, was compelled to use redoubled exertions in order

---

* Lieutenant Robert Keddle, of the 50th, died in this place, from the effects of a severe wound, which he received in France. He was interred with military honours, and a stone with a suitable inscription was placed over his remains.

to complete its numbers. The whole of the noncommissioned officers, with the band, and drums at their head, marched daily through the streets, tempting by most alluring baits those young fellows, who, struck with military ardour, were gazing and listening with wonder at all the fine speeches of the Serjeant*. Of the raw material there was abundant food for powder, and so many of the Hibernian youths were out of work that our battalion was soon filled up, and in the course of the summer we were quite prepared for any service.

From Enniskillen the Regiment marched to Londonderry, where they remained during the winters of 1815 and 1816.—While they were stationed in the garrison they were treated with

* The beating-up was a most enlivening affair; the horns and kettle-drums, together with the noise of various other instruments, made such a rattling through the town as kept the good people thereof wide awake, calling to the windows on every occasion a precious bevy of fair and blooming damsels, ready themselves to take on with any gallant gay Lothario, who might feel inclined to serve a campaign or two with them, in the field of Venus instead of that of Mars.

the utmost kindness by the people, who testified on all occasions the high respect in which they held the military profession; and those officers now alive who were at that period quartered there, can bear testimony to this record of the attention and generosity displayed by the inhabitants of that loyal and interesting city.

Several detachments from the Regiment were cantoned in various parts of the country, where they had but miserable accommodation. The officers thus situated led rather a solitary life, varied occasionally by the still-hunting expeditions, a species of service attended with much fatigue. Often have we travelled for miles over deserted tracts, and, after long continued wanderings, come perchance upon some spot where the illicit manufactory was in active work, and where every scheme and stratagem was used to avoid detection. Seized upon without resistance, the unfortunate people were paralysed with terror, and were captured together with their whiskey. Many were the wailings and sorrowful cries of these miserable creatures, thus dispossessed of all they were worth in the world; and it was pitiable to hear their wives and children in despair imploring for mercy, while the relentless hand of law held their husbands and fathers within its grasp.

It is much to be deplored that the King's troops should be employed in a duty of such a revolting nature, which brings them into hostile contact with the poor inhabitants of their own country; it is certainly no very agreeable, and it might be added, honourable employment, for any officer to be a gauger's whipper-in, or for his party to be the advanced guard of an excise officer, or deputy assistant carriers of potteen whiskey. We found it a most irksome, harassing and unpleasant service, the very recollection of which, even at this distance of time, is enough to make one shudder.

Whenever the approaching military were observed from the top of a distant hill, where scouts were posted to look out for the enemy, a signal was made to the dealers in the contraband, who were busily employed at their lawless calling, in a poor and roofless hut, situated in a remote corner of the mountain glen. From hill to hill the well known signal spread like wildfire, and long before the soldiers reached the spot, the chief performers were off, having previously destroyed or removed the whole apparatus of their trade, leaving not a vestige of whiskey or machinery behind. The loud shouting and hallooing of the terrified fugitives, while the gaugers thirsting for their prey gave chase, resounded among the heights. Knowing every pathway they soon outran the cunning excisemen, and by the best of generalship left them to measure back their steps, bewailing their ill fate, in thus losing their prize, that was almost within their clutches.

In order to fill up the intervals between these excursions, seeking for outlawed characters, hunting for robbers and highwaymen, or any other honest calling in that line, was the employment of the military. The duty of the officer was no sinecure; nor could he ever enjoy the quiet pillow, so frequent were the demands upon his time.

While the 50th was in Derry, Mr. Butler, of Grouse Hall, in the County of Donegal, was cruelly assassinated in front of his own hall door, by a noted villain named Magennis, who fired at him with deliberate aim, from a plantation before the house. Magennis, who had been engaged in other murders, bore a dreadful character, and in such horror was he held, that on hearing of the commission of this last diabolical act, that every well disposed and loyal person was willing to lend a hand in his capture, and an immense reward was offered for his apprehension. The troops of course were employed in this affair, and were out at all hours in pursuit of the outlaw, without success. For months he thus eluded the vigilance of the civil and military powers, outwitting them in their plans, and bidding defiance to their efforts to take (as he thought) his invulnerable body. Disguised in various costumes, he fled from place to place, as best might suit his purpose, perpetually changing his abode, from the remote villages to the mountains, and lying at times concealed in deep recesses of the wildest glen or rocky cavern, where assisted by his friends, (for, strange to say, this wicked man had friends!) he lay in privacy secure by day, while by night he prowled about the neighbourhood of his favorite haunts.

He was familiar with all the most inaccesible and unfrequented spots throughout the country, and with the trackless waste he was well acquainted. Being constantly on the watch, he was far distant from his pursuers at the very time they supposed him within their grasp. As soon as the soldiers appeared in sight, this daring robber, standing on a promontory, or ledge of rocks, and waving his hat in the air with loud shouts of defiance, would challenge the men to fire. At the next moment he would spring from the precipice, and mounting a hardy galloway, scour off in triumph to another hill; thus rendering useless all exertion to take him, and shewing the difficulty of making any man a prisoner in a country where the laws are not sufficiently respected, and where the vilest malefactor is screened and sheltered from their power by the populace, in whose neighbourhood the crimes have been committed.

Among those stationed at outquarters in Ennisshowen was Lieutenant John Winder Plunkett, of the 50th, who commanded a party in that district*. This officer, finding that the labours of his men for the apprehension of Magennis were in vain, and that it was a folly any longer to persist in the fruitless chace, consulted with the magistrates, who agreed with him in thinking that it would be better to proceed by way of stratagem. A few trustworthy fellows were accordingly despatched in disguise, conducted by faithful guides, who searched in various corners, with the view of

* Lieutenant I. W. Plunkett had served with honor to himself during greater part of the Peninsular war, but being reduced with the supernumerary Lieutenants of the 50th, he memorialized to be placed again on full pay. In consequence of his good conduct on former occasions, as well as in the capture of Magennis, he was, through the interest of Sir Robert Peel, appointed to the 25th, or Royal Borderers; with which regiment, he served some years in the West Indies, and died of fever in Demerara, in 1831, after becoming senior of his rank, deservedly regretted, not only by the 25th, but by all his old companions of the 50th.

taking the murderer by surprise. In consequence, however, of treachery, or false intelligence, even their exertions failed, and it was feared that he would at last escape, and thus avoid the punishment due to his enormous crimes.

Plunkett himself at length volunteered to make the dangerous attempt of seizing on the person of the lawless villain; and, as soon as he could get some clue, by which to ascertain his lurking place, he was resolved to proceed upon the enterprise. An opportunity was now at hand for carrying the plan into effect; for, one morning, while the Lieutenant was considering about the matter, a countryman disguised appeared suddenly in his room, and assured him, that, if due protection were afforded, he would conduct him to the place where Magennis was to sleep on the following night. Rejoiced at this welcome information, the officer at once closed with the man's proposal, and told him he would be ready to attend him in the morning.

At the appointed hour, the party was assembled, and, having to travel over a bleak and mountainous range of hills, the roads on which were intricate and bad, they did not arrive till midnight at the village, on the skirts of which they halted. The night was dark as pitch, the stillness of the grave prevailed throughout, and not even the smallest gleam of light was seen among the wretched group of dwellings. Every thing so far was favourable, and lest any treacherous design should lurk within the peasant's breast, our worthy cicerone was strictly guarded, and a loaded musket placed in the vicinity of his head. "Come now, my lads," whispered the Irishman, "move on in silence, you'll soon be at the spot;" on which they followed him on tiptoe; not even the barking of a dog was heard, to interrupt them. In a state of breathless caution they passed the cabins, from the window of one of which an ugly beldame peeped out her wizened face, and seeing the men, she quickly hobbled to the door; but the hag was in a moment seized, and told, in no very gentle terms, that if her ladyship made the slightest noise, her life would be the forfeit. This admonition caused Old Curiosity to quake so with fear, that her final exit would have speedily taken place had she remained in durance vile much longer. A man or two being left as body guards to her highness, the remainder moved on quietly down the street, when the guide, pointing to a poor and desolate hovel on the road, said, in a low voice, "The object of your search lies there." Measures were immediately taken to dispose the men in such a way about the cabin that no one could escape; sentries were placed at doors and windows, the soldiers were prepared with loaded arms to prevent a rescue, and nothing was left undone to secure their prey. On being informed of the room in which the guilty bandit lay concealed, Plunkett, a man of tried courage and great personal strength, quickly forced the outer door, and clearing all impediments he rushed onward through the passage, with a pistol loaded to the muzzle, made a rapid push into a small apartment, and perceived the outlaw extended on the bed; to spring like a hungry tiger on his prey, and put his weapon to the fellow's head, was the work of an instant. Magennis, armed to the teeth, and having for bedfellows a blunderbuss and brace of pistols, started up with horror, looking wildly and in fierce anger round, while he made a violent struggle to disentangle himself from the iron grip of Plunkett. The noise of these proceedings being the signal, the men without burst into the scene of action, when the ruffian, after making one last despairing effort to fire at the Lieutenant, and seeing that further resistance would be vain, surrendered to the party, delivering up his weapons to their brave commander. So completely was the villain taken off his guard, that he appeared almost paralysed with terror. Well aware that of mercy for his crimes there was none in store, he submitted with dogged looks to the men about him.

Astonished at the courage of his captor, he addressed him thus—"Sir, what rank are you in the 50th,"—"I am a Lieutenant," returned the officer. "Ah!" said Magennis, you ought to be General Plunkett, for having taken me."

The prisoner being pinioned, they marched him from the village, and, on the following day, he was safely deposited in the county goal. Thus was this notorious criminal taken in his bed, through the intrepid conduct of one individual, after the ineffectual efforts of many well-armed men. He was executed at Lifford, in a few months after. The unfortunate man, who acted as guide to the captors, was, in a short time, barbarously murdered by his countrymen.

CHAPTER XXII.

Being ordered to join the Regiment in the West Indies, I proceeded for that purpose from Albany Barracks, in the Isle of Wight, to Cowes, the 21st of November, 1820.—On the morning of the 22nd, the troops intended for the same destination embarked on board of the John Rickards, a fine ship, the captain of which, John Ward, was an excellent seaman, as well as a kind and amiable character. The detachments were composed of men belonging to the Royal Artillery, and 50th, 58th and 92nd regiments; all commanded by Major Henry Pierce, R.A.—

In consequence of the unfavourable state of the wind, the ship remained at anchor in the roads. The officers employed this interval in making further preparations, as well as in amusing themselves in the best way they could, some in wandering along the sandy beach, others in sauntering about the streets, and not a few in rambling through the country in various directions, exploring the beauties of the island.

On the morning of the 25th, the wind coming round to N. E., signal was immediately made, when with hasty steps we all repaired to the boats lying at the sea-beach, ready to convey us on board. In a little time the embarkation was completed, and about noon we were under way, standing down channel with a lively breeze, and a fine clear day. The bustle and commotion, incident to the beginning of a long passage, the stowing away of animated and inanimate lumber, with a train of other preparatory measures, were attended with the confusion and noise that generally takes place on such occasions, and it was not until we had got pretty well out to sea that matters subsided into something like good order and regularity.

The cabin was not much better than those narrow prisons usually are in the West India Merchantmen, but afforded tolerable head room to those who were not descended from a race of giants. The berths, or cupboard looking dens, intended to do the duty of sleeping places, on either side, were hammered up in a very rude style, without regard to comfort or convenience, presenting nothing whatever to allure to peaceful slumber the unfortunate being who was doomed to be incarcerated in them. Their odour was not exactly of a kind to rival that of the rose; such as they were, however, we had no alternative; a hammock suspended from the ceiling of the cabin would of two evils have been by far the least.

The officers were all a cheerful and good tempered set of men, each resolved to contribute his mite to the general stock of harmony; and thus assist to lessen the miseries that form unavoidably part and parcel of a shipboard life. Politely speaking, the fair ladies ought to have been first alluded to. Those whom we were so fortunate as to have for our companions, were well disposed to lend their aid in promoting whatever might tend to relieve the tiresome voyage. We could not therefore fail of being as happy as mortals could expect, under all the circumstances.

While passing the Needles, the pilot took his leave, burthened with numerous epistles and billet doux, to wives and sweethearts. We gave many a longing lingering look to his weather-beaten skiff, as it glided swiftly to the shore, viewing it as the last connecting link of that chain which bound us to Old England; but now alas! to be severed, while we remained under mournful feelings, which the bright aspect of surrounding things could hardly dissipate.

It was beautiful to behold, on that sunny day, the prospect on either side, whether we looked to the green hills of the Isle of Wight, or on the rich and varied scenery along the coasts of Hants and Dorset. Sailing at the rate of six or seven knots, we rapidly bounded through the water, and, bearing away to the south-east, in a few hours we cleared the English Channel.

By this time we began to experience certain very uncomfortable qualms, felt more or less by landsmen and sailors on their first invasion of the ocean. Gay and jocund looks were speedily changed into those of a more sickly character, the unpitied and unpitying malady, as the sea got rough, spreading its influence around. As for the griffins, or young adventurers, they vanished in silence to the lower regions, betaking themselves to their proper dens, where they lay perdue, meditating on their hapless fate; and, in a situation bordering on despair, were indifferent as to whether they went to the bottom of the deep, or were dismissed from the world by a shorter road. It is wonderful how soon the ardour of even the most ambitious hero is cooled by a bout of sea-sickness; the frame and spirit are paralysed, and all the energies of mind and body are lying prostrate, and he cares not a farthing for himself, or any human being. The worst of it is, no one has compassion on the wretched victim, and though he may seem absolutely in a dying state, the healthy and older hands only laugh or grin at his distress; shaking their contented sides, while they cruelly prescribe for the unhappy patient a fat mutton chop, or a wedge of greasy bacon. For the smallest spot of solid earth upon which to set one's foot, even though it were in a barren wilderness, the wealth of India would with gladness be exchanged, and, in bitterness of heart, the meanest reptile that ever crawled upon the surface of dry land becomes an object of envy.

Our gallant bark still ploughed her way through the restless and sparkling waters, bearing the faint and the light-hearted, the joyful together with the sad, onward to the warm and renovating atmosphere of southern regions. Even when our calamities were at their worst, there was always something to keep us from sinking into total despondency. Among other resources against care and ennui, there was the amusing society of a gentleman, named

Charles, our worthy surgeon, a stout, broad shouldered Milesian. He was the drollest fellow imaginable, of such infinite humour that he not only was the means of banishing the blue devils from those who were in health, but of raising the spirits of the sick and downcast. In short he was a genius that could keep the table in a roar.

We could not by any means get on without the Doctor, who, by his comicalities and racy mirth, has restored more patients than hundreds of his drenching brotherhood have done, by all their quackery, nostrums, pills and boluses. This jolly son of Esculapius had all the ready wit and quaint originality of his countrymen. By his songs, anecdotes and stories, the tedium of many a wintry night upon the deck was pleasantly beguiled. These were indeed sufficient to dispel the grievous thoughts of even the most miserable ascetic that ever pined away his days in cell or hermitage. Poor Charles ended his career in Jamaica, where he fell a victim to the yellow fever, and his brother officers were thus deprived of a social companion, and society of a good-natured and estimable member.

Biscay, with all its stormy attributes, now stared us wildly in the face, and shortly we were rolling on its waves, with nothing to relieve the prospect. We, fortunately, escaped this time any very tempestuous weather, being reminded only now and then, by sundry awful lurches, (to the total overthrow of tables and contents), that we were still in blustrous latitudes, and that we could not hope to cross this noted bay without some little tossing, and a brush or two from one of those gales for which it has so long been famed. Ground and lofty tumbling, as well as other gymnastics, sufficient to educate the novice for a trial of skill in that branch of science, holding on by ropes, a somerset or two, intermingled with a game at all fours, were consequently, in their turn, the most general occupations of the landsmen; while, at the dinner table, the farce that was occasionally exhibited was quite as good as anything that Mathews could perform, and could not fail to excite the risible faculties of a stoic.

When quietly seated round the festive board, during a lull, or while the sea was calm, there was nothing but "eat, drink, and be merry;" but, presently, comes on the old work of pitching and rolling. By one tremendous lurch, the company are thrown upon their beam-ends, all make a grasp at the table, which is followed by a pull at the cloth; then comes on the tug of war,—chairs, stools, benches, give way from their moorings, in consequence of the violent shock, accompanied by a column of plates, dishes, mugs, and glasses, with a long train of crockery, and our stock of eatables, all are mingled up together, and scattered about in every direction. A platter of potatoes is flung into the lap of the unlucky genius who has been endeavouring to rescue a leg of mutton; a piece of salt junk is delivered up in exchange for some pickled pork; and thrice happy the wight, who, in trying to save his own bacon, gains possession of a huge ham that flies most lovingly to his arms. Soup and gravy are distributed in profuse showers upon the sprawling gastronomes, who with open mouths engulf the savoury fluid, and ruefully glancing upwards, survey with wistful eyes the precious morsels, flying to and fro in mid air, to tantalize their hungry maws, rendering more keen the bitter misfortune which has thus so cruelly deprived them of cherished joys, now dissipated like the morning dew. Meanwhile the illfated masticators, so lately floored, not daring to let go the ring bolts and table legs which they most affectionately clasp, lie scrambling with all the appendages of bed and board coming in awful contact with their devoted heads; too happy, if perchance, amid the fearful chaos, they can be permitted to gnaw the tough and stringy junk, or enter into discussion with a flinty biscuit, seasoned by a ravenous appetite, the sauce a la mode with all campaigners of ancient and modern times.

So much for a dinner at sea. The drama brought forward while in the enjoyment of the beverage that "cheers but not inebriates," was much of the same character, whenever our good ship thought proper to recommence her antics, and comfort, like riches, "made unto herself wings and flew away," leaving her shipmates to weather it out in the best manner they were able during the period of her absence.

After doubling Cape Finisterre the weather became remarkably fine, and we began to experience the genial influence of a milder atmosphere. About the 4th of December, we approached the latitude of Madeira; the nights were beautiful and light, the stars also appearing with a brilliancy we had not before observed. While the winter in England was setting in with all its accustomed severity, we were throwing off our warm clothing, and getting the awnings and wind sails in readiness to guard against the effect of extreme heat. On the 8th, at daylight, land was seen from the mast head, which upon close, inspection proved to be that of the above island, bearing S. E. by S., and distant about twenty miles. The wind being contrary, we made but little way, beating off and on. sometimes becalmed, with the sails flapping idly about the masts and yards. In this wearisome situation, without any thing whatever to vary the dull sameness, we were glad to embrace the first opportunity that might present itself of making an attack upon our neighbours of the deep. The idlers, therefore, began to try their hand at a little amusement in that line. The appearance of some turtle, floating on the surface of the water, induced Captain Ward to lower the jolly boat, into which Ensign Ross and three expert sailors immediately leaped, pushing off at once with the intention of breaking in upon the slumbers of these drowsy animals, and, if possible, of introducing one or two of them to the acquaintance of the gentlemen on board.

Arriving at the spot where the fish were basking in the sun, they made an ineffectual effort to get one of them into their hands; and, soon after, they were seen tugging away lustily at the oar, on their return to the ship. They had unfortunately neglected to stop the hole by means of which the boat was to be drained, the water had gradually entered before they had perceived the error, and the boat was filling rapidly. There was no time to be lost; with every nerve and sinew the anxious crew leaned firmly to their work; but, being in a swamping state, they moved slowly through the water. By a miracle at last they gained their vessel, up the sides of which the exhausted men were hardly able to clamber. It was with difficulty they got on deck, thankful that they had so narrowly escaped a watery grave.

While we were off Madeira Captain Ward was desirous of complying with the wishes of the officers, by landing them, but the violent surf on the beach being likely to endanger us in the attempt, and the wind being light and baffling, it was found impossible to accomplish the desired object.

On the 14th of December we discovered the Island of Palma, bearing S. W. The famous Peak of Teneriffe was likewise observable. In a few days, we got within the influence of the Trade Winds, blowing regularly throughout the year, between N.E. and N.W. The deck now became agreeably cool, in consequence of the awning being spread, and our rate of sailing being generally six, seven, or eight knots, with a fine steady breeze, under every stitch of canvass we could bear, we generally ran from a hundred and fifty to two hundred miles in the twenty four hours. The only remarkable event that happened on the passage took place about this time, which nearly proved fatal to one of the men. A soldier of the 92nd being accused of theft, and fearing the shame and punishment that might ensue, formed the desperate resolution of throwing himself overboard. He accordingly jumped from the main shrouds into the sea, and, not being able to swim, he dropped fast astern. The ship, which was going at the rate of six knots, was hove to, and the jolly boat was immediately lowered, into which three of the crew threw themselves, and pulled in the direction pointed out by those on board. In consequence of a heavy swell, they could not succeed in finding the proper course, and every possible means of saving the poor fellow would have failed, had not Providence enabled him to float, until the boat was at last brought to his side, when they picked him up at about three hundred yards from the vessel, into which he was hauled in a state of complete exhaustion from fatigue and terror, after being more than twenty minutes in the water.

The nights in those latitudes were truly splendid, the brightness and clear silvery light of the moon, (now in the full), far outshining the usual appearance of that luminary in the temperate zone. The weather continued delightful, and for many days the sails remained unchanged, the seaman's life being almost a sinecure.

Protected from the intense heat, by the shade which the awnings afforded, our proceedings, whether for amusement or otherwise, were all conducted on the deck. The soldiers, sailors, and women, assembled there after sunset, as well as on the gangways, in order that they might, during the cool refreshing hours, have a little bit of sport in the way of dancing. Reels and hornpipes were the most prevailing favourites, and, to the music of a fife and bagpipes, they tripped it on the plank with no small degree of spirit. In these the Scottish lasses displayed a very good share of cleverness, and it was quite amusing to behold with what vanity as well as delight not a few of these merry Northerns footed it away, with all their heart and soul, untiring and untired, to the tune of the Cameronian Rant. The tars enjoyed the fun, and seemed completely in their element while figuring off in the pas-seul, or reeling it with the ladies. One of these damsels, in particular, a comely and laughter-loving wench, from the banks of the Clyde, known by the appellation of Dumbarton Mary, was in truth the picture of good humour. With rosy cheeks, and a brace of dark eyes, she had rather an interesting appearance, when in her tartan dress, and with stockingless feet, she gave them a specimen of the Highland fling.

Singing was also going forward, not only on the forecastle but on the poop, where our worthy medico had a knot of pleasant fellows seated round him, listening to the ditties by which he entertained them. Long yarns were spun, and every thing was put in requisition, so that the night was pretty well curtailed, when unwillingly each withdrew to dream of the day's adventure.

To celebrate the invasion of Father Neptune's empire, or, in common parlance, crossing the Line, preparations were actively made on all hands, and the usual as well as oft repeated ceremony was duly performed. This ridiculous mummery began at an early hour, and continued, with its noises, uproar, and buffoonery, to a late period of the day; drunkenness and excessive rioting reigned throughout the vessel;—sailors and soldiers were in one general state of disorder and intoxication. The custom, though of long standing, appears to have no other tendency than that of producing tumult and confusion amongst the crew, and is one of those absurdities that ought long ago to have been abolished.

In consequence of these unmeaning and dangerous proceedings, a private of the Royal Artillery, named Wailey, was found dead in his berth, on the following morning. Upon examination of his body by the Surgeon, it appeared that the unfortunate man drank to such excess of strong rum, that, having lain down and covered himself, he soon got suffocated, from the powerful effects of the liquor. He afforded an unhappy instance of the fatal consequences of intemperance, as well as of the evil that arises from that abominable practice to which he prematurely fell a victim.

On the 3rd of January, 1821, after being thirty six days at sea, intelligence of *land in sight* was joyfully heard by all on board, and towards noon, the small Island of Descada, in the Carribbean Sea, was plainly discernable on our larboard quarter, bearing W. S. W., and distant about twenty five miles. Every one arose and got on deck as quick as possible, in order to feast their eyes upon this most agreeable and welcome prospect. Directly a head further appearances of land presented themselves, and Guadaloupe soon became distinct; the lofty mountain of La Souffriere rising abruptly above the foreground, the nearest point of which was not more than four miles off.

In the course of the forenoon we came in sight of His Majesty's Frigate, Tribune, Captain Willoughby, which had been for some months cruizing about in this latitude. Our gallant ship bore up for the frigate, which had made a previous signal for that purpose, and on arriving close the troops and seamen gave her three hearty cheers. The tars who manned the yards of the Tribune returned the salute by a peal of loud huzzas, while their band, at the same time, in most excellent style played "Rule Britannia."

Our sails were filled, and once more steering on our course, the frigate bore away in a superior manner, giving us as we parted, "The girl I left behind me."

From the 8th to the 10th we lay becalmed off Cape Tiberon, the south-east point of St. Domingo, and on the evening of the latter day a fine breeze springing up, we made so good a run in the night time, as to bring up our loss, and, as we went at the rate of from eight to nine knots, St. Domingo was far astern by day light.

At a very early hour we were hailed by the cry of land in sight, and presently the Blue Mountains of Jamaica were distinctly visible on the lee bow. Rejoiced at these good tidings we continued on the deck, anxiously looking out, with the hope of being safely moored in the course of the evening; these hopes were fortunately realized, for the wind being steady, and blowing in our favour, we soon gained the east end of the island.

About ten A. M. we arrived off Port Morant, and, scudding along under all the canvass we could carry, cleared Yellah's point by two o'clock.

Nothing could be finer than the appearance of the island. As we closed in towards the coast the most splendid and romantic scenery opened to the eye, as we passed each headland, while the rich and varied country, bordering on the mountains, enlivened by the luxuriant cane fields, together with innumerable trees and wide plantations, formed on the whole a prospect of exceeding beauty.

By five P. M. we made Port Royal, and soon after dropped anchor in the harbour.

The Pilot we had taken on board was now to his very great joy discharged. He had no great relish for the blowing he had got, and seemed miserable while he was in the chilly regions of our vessel. All the time that we were panting and puffing from the heat, and trying to get into every hole and corner from the sun, our sable commodore said " it was berry cold day", and shivering in every limb, like a navigator at the pole, crouched in from a breeze that felt as though it were coming from a furnace. When blacky first put his foot upon the gangway he looked about him with an air of some authority, and standing by the helm assumed no little consequence.

It was nearly sunset when the anchor was let go, which operation was no sooner performed than some boats came along side, bearing certain officials, who in their exercise of pretended duty, or curiosity, commenced prying about with rather an important air; among them were idlers and loungers not a few, who, with the usual preface of "I hope I don't intrude", began rummaging all about the ship, poking into every hole and corner for stale newspapers, old magazines, or any other chance provender for their inquisitive appetites. Nothing escaped the notice of those gentry, who with open mouthed avidity poured forth a whole volley of questions, about affairs in general, in that country from whence we came. Having fully satisfied their minds that there was no more to be explored, the intermeddlers vanished, previously helping themselves quite coolly to any little matters that were thrown about, of course of no use in the world to the late owners. By this time there was scarcely any twilight, darkness suddenly coming over the face of every object, while at the same time impenetrable mist overspread the wide and placid harbour; as there was not the slightest breath of wind, the land breeze not yet being felt, a most oppressive heat and closeness produced on the new comers a suffocating effect, that made them not in the least desirous of resuming their berths below.

CHAPTER XXIII.

Some of the officers, of whom I was one, went ashore at Port Royal, to enjoy an hour or two's recreation, and to stretch their legs, a luxury which it may well be imagined was most acceptable to them, after being cooped up within the narrow precincts of a few planks nailed together, and with only the interminable marine view as a relief to the mind.

We entered a tavern, in the lower part of the town, where we indulged in a copious draught, known by the name of porter cup, an excellent and refreshing beverage, made of Madeira wine, Port, and other ingredients, and which I commend to the notice of any traveller who may hereafter travel that way. This tavern was kept by a facetious and eccentric character, well known by the appellation of Johnny Feron, a sort of French adventurer. His house was generally well frequented by strangers, who, during the period that they remain within his care, he, by means of an exorbitant bill, relieves of the troublesome burthen of any loose cash by which they may be overloaded.

The house of this wily Frenchman was crammed full from top to bottom of soldiers and sailors, carousing, smoking and revelling. The galleries were occupied by a noisy crew, who with loud and obstreperous mirth made the slender fabric ring. Upstairs and down, the landlord with his train of dusky waiters were running to and fro, so many were the calls for the attendance of these worthies; the tongues of the bells chimed in with that of their master, while a garrulous jargon was kept up, that made us gladly take leave of this Pandemonium for the more tranquil regions of the ship; we therefore hastened to the beach, where a boat was in readiness to convey us on board.

The hotel, (which from the number of its customers was entitled to that designation,) was a light and flimsy tenement, and, like other buildings throughout the island, was but a mere piece of framework, lathed or boarded in, and having verandas and jalousies, painted in various gaudy colours. In consequence of the prevalence of storms and hurricanes, the elevation in these cases is never beyond the first floor, from whence project a range of galleries, supported by the pillars of the colonnade below. The whole arrangement of the slender edifice is such, that any inconvenience arising from the heat and other effects of such a climate is but slightly felt.

The town of Port Royal, (situated, as is well known, on that remarkable strip of sand that forms the eastern barrier of Kingston harbour) has had many awful visitations, being so often destroyed by earthquakes, and as often rebuilt upon the ruins, that it is fit only for those who, being tired of their lives, would venture on the chances of a new and summary mode of making their final exit. However, the importance of the station as a naval depôt, as well as that of the works commanding the entrance of the bay, have outweighed all other considerations, and have induced the government at home to keep so strong a garrison there, that the remnant of a town is yet preserved, although from past experience one might expect that desolation and tottering walls would be its only monument.

The long narrow bank, which is terminated at its point by a strong battery, is barren and unfruitful, presenting not the least vestige of cultivation, or other object pleasing to the eye, with the exception of some straggling cocos, standing like sentinels at the water's edge, and the scattered tumble-down looking houses, with many indications of decay, forming a sort of close irregular street, of which, taverns, gaming houses, and other receptacles of vice, are the most prominent features.

On the following morning, at day-break, we jumped upon deck, with all the eagerness and impatience of a bevy of gaol birds on emancipation from their prison house. Rowing across that wide and beautiful bay, we hauled to, along side of the wharf at Kingston, where, on landing, the several fellow travellers separated, each for the quarters to which he was bound. Accompanied by Ensign William Ross, of the 50th, I proceeded direct through the principal street to the house of Mr. Smith, a respectable merchant, under whose hospitable roof many officers of the garrison found a cordial welcome. Our friend was enjoying himself under the cool shade of his veranda, where he received us in an open and generous manner, and, arriving just in time for breakfast at the usual hour of six, we partook of an excellent repast, to which our morning excursion on the water enabled us to do sufficient justice.

The habitation of our worthy host was a pretty fair sample of those throughout the town, and, although not large, was commodious, and furnished in a style adapted to the climate; matting of split cane, or straw, instead of carpets, the chairs of cane, and every other article to correspond. Within the piazzas, on the ground-floor, were the store and offices, and, opening from the galleries above, were the several domestic chambers.

Without delaying to explore the geography of Kingston, we started about eleven for the barracks at Up Park Camp, in a sort of gig or cabriolet peculiar to the island, and arrived about twelve o'clock.—Here we found the 50th stationed, under the command of Lieut Colonel John Bacon Harrison, to whom having duly reported, we were handed over to the apartments allotted for our reception. The troops then in Jamaica were the 50th Colonel Harrison; 58th Colonel D. Walker; 61st Colonel Ryal; and the 92nd Colonel —; the 50th and 92nd, the latest comers, whose ranks diminished by the sickness of the last year were almost reduced to skeletons, were little better than the shadow of what they were at the time of landing.

Of the old 50th but few remained.—Completed before they sailed, to the full establishment, by a fine set of young men from the North of Ireland, they departed from that country in the highest state of order and equipment for this island, where they had not been stationed for many months when the most sickly season set in that for many years had been remembered.

Full of strength, and the vigour of youth, the new soldiers soon became the victims of disease; indulging immoderately perhaps in the pernicious rum, and ignorant of its baneful effects, they lay prostrate in dreadful numbers beneath the dreadful pestilence. So great a sacrifice of human life had not taken place in all our hardest battles combined together, and the oldest inhabitants here tried in vain to recollect a more severe and afflictive dispensation.—With regard to the officers, from the Colonel to the youngest Ensign, including staff, the greater number were carried away.*

* From the year 1819 to 1826, the 50th and 92nd lost 1409

Among the 50th, the fever broke out in July 1819. The 92nd Highlanders did not arrive until the early part of the summer in that year, and were therefore badly seasoned. Being a long time companions in the same brigade, the meeting between these corps was consequently joyous, and in order to celebrate the happy event they dined together in the camp. Sobriety of course was not a member of the party; and, as might well be expected, the

---

men, which is at the rate of 88 ℔ year each regiment, in the eight years.

The 33rd and 91st, from 1822 to 1829, (eight years,) lost 1036 men, or about 65 a year, each.

The 77th, from 1824 to 1829, (six years,) lost 433, or 72 men a year.

The 22nd and 84th, lost from 1826 to 1829, (three years,) 501, or 84 men a year, each regiment.

In Jamaica the most unhealthy months in the year are August and November, and the most healthy are May and June; in the former months the mortality is four times as great as in the latter months. Dividing the year into two equal parts, the "healthy season" may be considered as extending from February to July, the "unhealthy season" from August to January. The deaths in these two seasons are as ten to twenty-seven.

The seasoning, or period of severe mortality, generally occurs in the latter half of the year in which a regiment arrives.

hospital was not without its portion of the company on the ensuing day. Predisposed as the men in general were by former habits, as well as by frequent exposure to the nightly dews, the malady broke out with violence unparelleled among both regiments; from that period it raged throughout the island, sweeping all before it, and even among the civilians the mortality was unbounded.

In some localities the ravages were far more dreadful than in others; Up Park camp, Spanish town, Fort Augusta, and Stony hill were among the fatal number, and at a small place on Kingston harbour, called Greenwich, no human being could exist. In a fort erected there, upon a low and swampy piece of ground, a party of artillery had been posted, the whole of whom soon died; another was sent, but they followed their companions; and so rapidly did each in succession fall under the pernicious exhalations arising from this deadly spot that it was, at length, abandoned altogether.

On the list of those who perished was Colonel Charles Hill of the 50th, who, after beholding with grief the loss of nearly all his officers, was himself attacked while stationed at Fort Augusta. His mind and body were thoroughly exhausted, and the sufferings he underwent were, in themselves, enough to bear down a stronger man, but when the fatal illness came, he was indeed badly able to withstand its violent effects.

Alone as it were in the midst of pestilence and death, his fortitude was well nigh overcome by the affliction he was doomed to suffer, in following to the silent tomb, one after another, his friends and faithful companions in arms. It was, indeed, a trial too hard for the firmest mind to bear, and affected this estimable man so much, that, afterwards, he never held up his head.

Few were then remaining to pay the last and mournful tribute to his memory, but those few, with heartfelt sorrow, witnessed his interment, where so many of his soldiers had previously been laid. To perpetuate the worth of the excellent and gallant officer, a monument was erected, in the church at Kingston, where, although upon the marble was inscribed abundant testimony of his fame, an inscription far less perishable is deeply engraven on the hearts of *all* who had ever been under his command.

Colonel Hill was above forty years in the 50th, serving with them in every clime, and during every time of peril. Possessed of independance, he might long since have retired to the enjoyment of private life, but no,—the regiment was his home, the officers and soldiers were his family; with them he passed the flower of his life, with them he passed to an honorable tomb. An earnest desire for the welfare of his country, together with an ardent zeal in the service of his king, were the actuating motives by which he was influenced to the latest hour of his existence.

Up Park Camp is beautifully situated on an extensive piece of level ground, at the base of the Liguana mountains, enclosed by the prickly pear, and a great variety of flowering shrubs. The verdant plain is interspersed with numerous rich and valuable trees, whose luxuriant foliage has a brilliant and enlivening effect.

The spacious esplanade, upon which the barracks stand, is ornamented and embellished with all the taste displayed in the park of some noble mansion, while the magnificent hills, in the back ground, clothed to their summits with impenetrable wood, serve to heighten the grandeur of a scenery that stands unsurpassed by any thing to be met with in this habitable globe.

Notwithstanding the assemblage of lovely objects, which are presented on the face of this bright landscape, and however it may be a paradise in appearance, all its advantages are neutralized by its pernicious climate, and the camp, after all, is but a gilded mausoleum.

It is likewise morally impossible to enjoy existence in a place where so many annoyances must hourly be encountered, not only from the excessive heat, but from innumerable tormenting insects, and crawling things, that banish all repose, and interfere with every comfort which one might otherwise enjoy.

The report of a heavy piece of ordnance called us up at day break, and the performances commenced by the parade taking place soon after. During the breakfast hours, the spacious green, (then brown with heat,) before our quarters. presented some amusement to the gentlemen at the windows; for sundry maidens, with complexions that would rival Day and Martin, flocked about the settlement, vending their different wares, consisting of tawdry ornaments for the soldiers' wives, and fruits of luscious quality to tempt the officers.—Passing off their jokes and pleasantries, the sable fair-ones, (to use an Irishism), puffed up their goods, while they patiently endured the fire of a volley of oranges, which was discharged from the galleries at their lovely heads.

From eleven till twelve the second breakfast, answering to the Eastern tiffin, was ready in the mess-room, where a banquet was spread out that would have tickled the palate of a Nabob.—The remainder of the day till sunset was one unvarying round of dulness. Sometimes, however, strange as it may seem, the active game of cricket was engaged in, when, under a broiling sun, with jackets off, the characters in the sport seemed using their best efforts to end all their troubles by finding a speedy mode of exit.

Evening parade, at five, was the rallying point for a grand turn out; warlike evolutions, and the military music, in strains harmonious, attracted the fair and languid belles of Kingston. These fascinating daughters of Eve, while in graceful attitudes they lounged in curricle, or landau, cast many a bewitching look upon the gallant heroes thus honoured with their presence.

The rolling of the well known drum, at six, announced the hour of dinner, and round the board were soon collected the hungry candidates, for fame before the trenches, (quere, trenchers)? The happy votaries at the shrine of Epicurus were duly arranged in order of battle, and with Aldermanic science acted their parts, to the no small havoc of the quickly vanishing fare.

Were it possible to exercise the reasoning powers in this abominable furnace there was sufficient means of so doing; for a well stocked library of chosen books afforded a source of enjoyment, that, in any other situation would have been invaluable. But with the thermometer at 90° in the shade, and bright Sol nearly vertical, the faculties of the mind were almost paralysed, and as for the body, it was kiln dried with a vengeance.

Although the months of December and January are considered more temperate than any other throughout the year, the heat when we arrived was intolerable; and as for going out of doors in the middle of the day, it was in truth a melting concern. The sun being at its greatest power between nine o'clock and two in the afternoon, (the interval between the land and sea breeze,) during that time no one in his common senses would venture abroad. The most agreeable portion of the twenty four hours is about sunrise, when the oppressive effects of the sultry atmosphere are tempered by the fresh and balmy air of morning. The evenings, likewise, are pleasant and refreshing, and it is then that exercise and driving about are much enjoyed. The heavy dews at night are highly injurious, and an exposure to their influence is dangerous, if not fatal, particularly to the stranger, or newcomer, who, not being seasoned to all the vicissitudes of these torrid regions, becomes an unguarded victim to his inexperience.

One of the greatest evils attendant on a residence here is the constant thirst, arising from the extreme aridity of the climate, and the violent action of the Solar rays upon the human frame and constitution. The appetite is therefore in general slight, but the inclination to drink is excessive. Hence it is, that sangaree, swizzle, and other mixtures, not exactly in accordance with the rules and laws of the Temperance Society, are continually in requisition, and find their willing votaries at every hour. An old hard-going veteran, who had been tanned and roasted to a cinder, on being asked for his opinion of the country, replied, like a true Salamander, "O! 'tis the finest place in the world, because one is always thirsty, and there is always plenty to drink." The bacchanalian remark was true; for Madeira, Rum and Brandy, flow in copious streams from a fountain, whose source is never exhausted. From the table these liquids, with their accompaniments, are seldom, on any occasion, absent; and the custom of quaffing the intoxicating beverage, in draughts unlimited, is general throughout the length and breadth of all these sun-burnt islands.

The rains seldom fall, but when they do, it is in right earnest, descending with so much violence, that they have some resemblance to a second deluge, of which our puny showers at home can give no adequate idea. To be overtaken in one of them is an adventure of no common peril, and unless the traveller succeeds in a precipitate flight to some adjacent place of shelter, he is in a moment drenched as thoroughly as if he were dragged across a horse-pond.

An attack of fever is the certain consequence of getting wet, and remaining in that condition for the shortest time. Lieutenant Richardson of the 50th, an officer who had been much on service, going to Stony Hill, where he was quartered, was suddenly caught by a down-pour, which fell so unmercifully that in a minute or two he was completely soaked.

Having no place of refuge from the storm, he rode on quickly towards the mountain, at the foot of which there was a small tavern where the Lieutenant hastily alighted, and, without making any change in his apparel, he drank freely of some rum and water. The weather clearing up, he was anxious to arrive at his barracks before sunset, and therefore proceeded without much delay upon his journey, at the end of which he found himself quite dry. The effects of his imprudent conduct were soon evident, for the fatal malady got possession of his frame, and his life was terminated on the following day.

While the fever was at its height among the troops, Mrs. Ross, wife to Surgeon Baily Ross of the 50th, an amiable young woman, interesting both in manner and appearance, embarked in one of the traders bound for England; but scarcely had she left the island when a violent tempest drove back the ship, and cast her on the rocks to the eastward of Port Royal, where she went to pieces and became a total wreck. The passengers, however, with great difficulty, and after extreme sufferings, at length succeeded in getting safe ashore, to which, although with loss of all their baggage, they were thankful that they had escaped with their lives.

Poor Mrs. Ross, alone and unprotected, was ill prepared to meet the sudden and unexpected blow, and with her companions in misfortune, bereft of every thing but the clothes she wore, she returned again to Kingston.

Anxiety of mind, together with the hardships that she must have undergone, were too much for so delicate a frame, and before she could obtain another passage, she was seized with fever, and all her trials and sufferings were shortly ended. The sad event called forth the grief of those who had known the worth of this kind and gentle lady, who, in the bloom of youth, was thus cut down, like a fair and lovely flower, when her bright hopes of returning to her friends and country were about to be realized.

Kingston is a good sized town, situated on an inclined plane, sloping to the water side, where all the principal warehouses and the markets stand. The streets are regularly planned, intersecting each other at right angles, abounding in shops (or stores), well filled with all the varieties of European manufactures. The appearance of the town, in general, has something of a dull and sombre character, in consequence of the finery and other things being hidden within the stores, in the windows of which there is little or no display ;—the market, however is a lively place where the chattering and good-humour of the negro girls attract the observation of the stranger more than the rich and delicious fruit they carry in their baskets. The Hotels and boarding-houses were most expensive, their respective proprietors taking good care to make the unfortunate traveller or tourist disgorge most woefully.—The bill was usually in accordance with the inverse ratio of the conscience; of which latter commodity there being little or none, the length of the former, may easily be guessed at.—In fact one could not open one's mouth under a dollar, even if it were but a glass of porter, and the residence of a night made a wide breach in a month's pay, or caused a doubloon to look exceedingly foolish on the ensuing morning. Between black waiters, black chamber-maids, and the whole establishment of sable beauties, the work of fleecing was vigorously carried on, until the unlucky griffin was cajoled and shorn of his last penny.

From all that we could learn respecting the fair sex in Kingston, or of Jamaica at large, they were interesting and pretty; at least so much might be said of those who favoured us with their company on the parade at Up Park camp, while we passed in review before them. Accustomed as they are to a life of listless indolence and luxurious ease, they use but little exertion of mind or body throughout the day, and the enervating influence of the climate promotes a languishing effect in the manner, as well as in their attitudes, that is really very attractive. Beyond the limits of their well-shaded saloons, or closely screened balconies, they hardly ever move; there, gracefully reclined on couch or sofa, the lovely nymphs dream away the lazy hours; decked out in purest white, with ornaments most brilliant, they simper, smile, or perchance, by great exertions, may enter into converse, with some admiring youths, with whom it would be sacrilege to laugh. Dancing is their favourite amusement, and one which they enjoy with all their life and soul, considering their usual half torpid habits, this is a circumstance not easily accounted for, but so it is. Their energies seem to be all reserved for this their chief delight, and, during those hours when all around are wrapped in sleep, these happy fair ones linger in the ball-room, until Aurora, peeping through the jalousies, reminds them that their charms may suffer by comparison with her rosy beams. The pallid hue, which they soon acquire, is made still more like the lily by these nightly revels, while the total want of healthy exercise in the fresh and open air tends to perfect the fragile ensemble of a West India belle.

The male bipeds of the community must

not be overlooked, lest they might be haunted by the green-eyed monster. The planters, or those engaged in trade, together with the whole professional tribe, had their pens, (or country houses,) and in some sequestered dell or glade the modest mansion rises. Here they retired, after the heat and bustle of the day, to feast and ruminate upon the best of living.

Kingston was like a city of the plague from twelve at noon till six the following morning. Transacting their affairs in cooler hours, by sunset all were on the move, and, like the land crabs, journeyed in a body to the mountain districts, the money-changers driving to their rural homes, or to the military parade.

The burning heat of the town, although so near the water, is insufferable, and the creoles, however enured to it, feel its full effect.—They sink into drowsiness and apathy, lounging on the galleries, or before their shops, (I beg their pardon, *stores* I ought to say,) with their pedestals stuck up against the walls, or on the backs of chairs, and they keep up such an oscillating movement that a new comer would suppose they were making an experiment to discover the perpetual motion; on being addressed they lazily drawl out the words as if it were painful to articulate.

Spanish Town, to which there is a good road from Kingston, is situated on the unhealthy banks of the Cobre, and is perhaps one of the hottest ovens under the sun. Its chief importance is derived from the circumstance of the government house being there, and of its being the head quarters of a regiment. The 92nd Highlanders were stationed in the barracks at that time.

CHAPTER XXIV.

EARLY in February, at Kingston, I embarked in the brig Vittoria, Captain Ferrier, and, soon after, the vessel dropped down to the anchorage at Port Royal. Just before we got under way, a transport arrived from England, having on board a detachment for the garrison, consisting of drafts from the 50th and 58th depôts, under the command of Captain Mason of the former corps; the other officers were Lieut. Crofton and Assistant Surgeon Young of the 50th and Lieut. Skinner of the 58th. Wishing them all happiness, I returned to my own ship, which immediately put to sea. On the 4th we were off the Island of Cuba, and passed the Grand Caymans at midnight. The weather was fine and the wind blowing fresh from the eastward. We made cape Antonio, the western extremity of Cuba, and in the course of the day stood away to the northward, in order to clear the Colorado shoals on the N.W. of the Cape. While sailing through the Gulf of Mexico, the sun was extremely hot, and very little wind stirring. We caught two small sharks with the line and hook, and having some slices fried for dinner, found them very tough, as well as strong and unsavoury to the taste.

A fine pleasant breeze springing up, we steered in shore, making the northern coast of Cuba, and about noon, the day being remarkably clear, the hills of that island were distinctly seen at the distance of twenty miles.

The wind becoming easterly on the 12th, we continued beating about the Mexican sea, and between the southern extremity of the North American coast and the east end of Cuba. Towards evening we were off the Havannah, and in view of the fortress and castle of the Moro, protecting the entrance into the harbour. Assisted by a strong current we passed a considerable distance to the eastward of the Havannah, and, as the current was running three and four knots, aided by a smart S.E. breeze, we hoped to clear the Florida passage in a few days. Before we got within the influence of the Gulf stream, we were hailed by a strange sail to leeward, which fired a few shots to bring us to. She immediately sent a boat, manned with some desperate looking villains, for the purpose of rummaging the ship. Having obtained all that they required, among which was a portion of our fresh stock, the suspicious visitor bore away to the westward. She proved to be an independent cruizer, named the Confidante of Buenos Ayres, and was one of the insurgent privateers by which those seas were infested. Fortunately, a heavy swell and threatening change of wind coming on, were the means of causing the pirate to sheer off suddenly, otherwise, we might not have escaped on such easy terms from his clutches.

With a fine spanking breeze at S.E. we were rapidly sailing through the Gulf; the weather continued moderate, and the sea tolerably smooth. On the 15th we entered the narrowest part of the straits, about sixteen miles from the shores of the Bahamas.

February the 16th and 17th, clearing the Gulf, we launched into the Great Western ocean, and underwent a series of desperate weather, attended with squalls and rain. The wind being right astern, our little brig was in the utmost danger of getting pooped by the heavy rolling sea, which was driving us along. The dead lights were stove in as fast as they were secured, and the decks were washed from stem to stern. In this way, at the rate of between eight and ten knots, we were scudding under close-reefed topsails. On the 18th and 19th, there was no improvement whatever in the state of things, although the wind was still blowing in a favorable direction. We were at this time in the latitude of Charleston, North Carolina.

Matters continued much in the same state

till the 27th, when, at midnight, the dark and stormy appearances of the sky gave indubitable indications of an approaching hurricane from the Northwest. At three in the morning, while running at six knots, the ship suddenly broached to, the foretopsail was torn off the yard arm, and, soon after, the main topsail and jib were literally rent like brown paper, flying in ribbons about the masts.

The whistling noise through the rigging, together with the rattling of blocks and sheets, was really dismal, and the gale kept encreasing with such fury as had never been witnessed by the oldest mariner on board. The sun had set, on the preceding evening, with all those direful omens which are the well known forerunners of bad weather, while the black and lowering clouds, banked up in wild and broken masses, foretold its continuance.

Daylight, so anxiously looked out for, disclosed to our view the horrors by which we were surrounded. The tempest had by this time gained a degree of violence that can be conceived only by such as have voyaged in those latitudes, and at its mercy our poor weather-beaten ship, labouring and struggling against its fury, was allowed, (or rather forced), to drift considerably off her course, in consequence of the helm being dismantled and unmanageable. With elastic bound she rose on the top of each successive wave, then fell as nobly into the furrows, seeming as if despair had given her strength, while the waters with dreadful noise rushed past her quivering sides, and with their accumulated weight occasionally broke upon the decks, sweeping off bulwarks, boats, and every timber on the gangways; while all her masts, yards and spars aloft, bent and strained beneath the fearful blast that howled in dismal gusts around. The sea, agitated into white and boiling foam, was running mountains high, and its angry surface presented a most desolate and wintry aspect.

Throughout this day the hurricane raged without the slightest intermission, every now and then a ponderous billow, coming with the force of a battering-ram upon her broadside, made the little sea-boat tremble to her very keel. She soon began to leak in all her seams, and the crew, harassed and fatigued, relieved each other by turns, while lashed to the pumps they worked incessantly. All but the seamen were down below, none daring to venture from those regions even for a moment. Pent up within the dark and gloomy limits of the cabin, we remained in awful durance, scarcely giving utterance to a word; our silence occasionally disturbed by a waterfall, tumbling through the sky-light, or companion hatchway, and leaving the steerage and cabin floor in a perfect deluge. Such a day of misery was never passed; and the Captain, who had been under many a stiff norwester, confessed that a gale like this he had not before encountered. The sun set with the same forbidding aspect as on the day preceding, and the night began without the slightest prospect of a change;—every one seemed to be in a state of hopeless despair, and were it not for that buoyancy of spirit, which is natural to man under every circumstance, none would have been capable of the least exertion.

The darkness in which we were involved rendered our situation more deplorable than ever, and without any thing whatever to cheer or comfort us, the most painful forebodings weighed down upon all on board. The Mate, Mr. Grant, however, a hearty good-humoured sailor, a man inured to danger in every form, kept us alive; encouraging the drooping passengers and crew, he never for an instant gave way to useless repining, but exerted himself as far as he could do under circumstances so trying. "With plenty of searoom, and a good ship," he said, "there was nothing to apprehend;" and his example did more to inspire the men with energy to work than any other means could possibly have accomplished. A little before midnight the utmost climax of the tempest seemed to have arrived, and it was hoped a change would soon take place. Grant, after drinking a glass of grog, and wrapping a pilot's frock about him, went on deck, for the purpose of looking out for something favourable; and we impatiently waited his return, as the harbinger of good tidings.

For a considerable time, we heard nothing but the ceaseless thunder of the wind and waves. At length, Captain Ferrier, fearing that something must have happened to detain the Mate, called out for him, from the top of the companion ladder, but no answer was received; the call was repeated throughout the ship, still no reply. Ferrier now perceived that the capstan head, dripstone, and taffrel rail were cleared away, since he was on deck before, and he soon guessed the fate of his unfortunate officer. Grant was last seen by a man at the pumps, holding on by the capstan; but in a moment one of the tremendous seas broke over the ship, with an overwhelming force, and washed the illfated seaman into the deep, together with the solid timber upon which he leaned.

All danger seemed for the present set aside, in our regrets for this worthy shipmate. He was a most skilful and zealous man, always at his post, engaged in every active business of the vessel, and unwearied in his duty in the hour of danger.

Immediately after the occurrence of this melancholy accident, the Captain, on glancing round the horizon, observed symptoms of an abatement of the gale; the wild commotion of the elements seemed to be gradually subsiding, and the weather-wise mariner expressed his opinion that, in a few hours, the wind would become so moderate as to enable him to steer his proper course. This welcome information was fully realized, for, even before it was expected, this change took place. Suddenly relieved from inevitable shipwreck, the crew began to work with fresh alacrity, and the tattered remnant of our sails was speedily put in order for instant use; so that by good exertion, crippled as she was, the ship moved slowly onward, and after sunrise, on the 1st of March, was making tolerable way, before a steady breeze and a comparatively smooth sea; dashing up the spray from beneath her bows, with a noise that sounded like the sweetest music in our ears.

Our party assembled at the breakfast table in high glee and spirits; a state of mind far different from that in which we had been for several days. Our late probation of abstinence had reduced us to a very slender compass, we therefore, set to with a goût that could not be imparted by Messrs. Harvey or Burgess, and the coarse though solid fare was rapidly devoured; the attacks were boldly made, and the enemy, in the shape of bare bones and empty platters and cups was quickly put to flight.

Three beside the Captain made up the number of our company in the cabin, one of whom, an old Scotch gentleman, who had made his fortune in the Plantations, was retiring in the evening of his days, to spend his money in his own country. He had been the greatest part of his life in Jamaica, and seemed to have lost all recollection of the period when he first left home; suffering under infirmity of body, and from the effect of climate, he was reduced to a very indifferent state of health.

The other passenger was a gentleman, whose intellect was rather out of order; in fact, when he was put on board the Vittoria at Port Royal, he was quite deranged, being held in charge of two men, who with difficulty prevented him from jumping into the sea. However, he cooled a little afterwards, although, during the whole voyage, he displayed many wild symptoms. While the hurricane lasted he kept close to his berth, and was in such a dreadful state of terror, that he did nothing but call out every moment that we were going down, and he fancied the violent concussion of the waves against the ship to be no other than our contact with the bottom of the ocean, at which he supposed we had arrived. Nothing whatever, but extreme longing for gain, could have induced any one in his common senses to admit such an unruly character into the ship, at all events without the very necessary appendage of a straight waistcoat. The poor man himself, however, was much to be pitied, for he was the victim of many serious trials. The vessel in which he sailed for the West Indies, a few years back, took fire, while lying becalmed off Cape Tiberoon, and was burnt to the water's edge. He narrowly escaped destruction, being obliged to leap overboard, and with others was rescued from the devouring element.

The fright caused by the awful situation in which he had been placed, affected his mind at the time, but not so as materially to affect his reasoning powers; he had wisdom enough left to seek for comfort with a blooming partner, a planter's daughter; which circumstance, it was said, rather increased than diminished the malady.—This fair lady died, and to prove his estimation of the married state, he took to his arms a second helpmate, with whom he resided at an estate called Vere. Misfortune still pursued the unhappy man; the last companion of his woes and joys followed her predecessor to the tomb, and the mourning widower, who was no admirer of the creed of Malthus or Miss Martineau, was left to go a third time, like another Cœlebs, in search of a wife. If to have been burned out of a ship, and enjoyed the felicity of having had two wives, with the chances of getting his head again into the noose were not enough in all conscience to qualify a man for Bedlam, it would be a difficult matter to find out what could effect that desirable object. Such was the case of our friend, of uxorious memory and to the disasters of his campaigns, we were perhaps indebted for the pleasure of his society on the passage home.

The dark and threatning aspect of the weather, for the rest of the voyage, gave us no reason to doubt that the Equinoxial gales would support their usual character, and that Boreas would attend us to our destined harbour.

Continuing our course across the great Atlantic, we got into soundings about the eighteenth of March, and were off the S.W. coast of Ireland, but the atmosphere being thick and hazy, the land was not discernible. Keeping the lead in active operation, we slowly though cautiously approached the Channel. The weather cleared up on the 21st, when with a fine breeze from the S.W. we gained the Lizard, at an early hour, and having made a capital run past the Eddystone and Needles, were compelled to heave to, off the S. Foreland, in consepuence of a dense fog. Signals were made for a pilot, which were answered by a rough looking member of that tribe pulling up, and boarding us. The night set in dark, but the moon shining out towards twelve o'clock, we stood away for the Downs, illumined by her light; and came to anchor about three in the morning of the 22nd of March 1821, after a stormy passage of seven weeks and two days.

On our getting moored, some Deal boats crowded round the ship, and their crews made the most extravagant demands for their services. Impatient to set foot on shore, after being so long caged up in my floating prison, I gladly embraced the opportunity, and agreeing to give the rapacious fellows a guinea for a two miles pleasuring on a wintry morning, my goods and chattels were gathered from the hold, and being tumbled into a boat, were soon followed by their master. We then shoved off, and I bade adieu to the shattered brig, and strange as it may appear, not without some feelings of regret. Rowing for about an hour against a head wind and strong tide, we hurried through the surf and brought to on the sandy beach of Deal, and with joy unspeakable, I once more found myself on the shores of happy England.

THE END.

BURY ST. EDMUND'S:
PRINTED BY T. C. NEWBY, ANGEL HILL.

Milton Keynes UK
Ingram Content Group UK Ltd.
UKHW041210231023
431175UK00004B/514

9 789354 5081